SEXUAL SINS OF THE BIBLE

EVERYTHING YOU WANTED TO KNOW, BUT WOULDN'T ASK!

All scripture quotations are taken from the New Kings James
Version of the Bible, unless otherwise indicated.

SEXUAL SINS OF THE BIBLE
EVERYTHING YOU WANTED TO KNOW, BUT WOULDN'T ASK!

ISBN: 0-9744519-1-6

SEXUAL SINS OF THE BIBLE

EVERYTHING YOU WANTED TO KNOW, BUT WOULDN'T ASK!

By

Pastor Louis Smith

TABLE OF CONTENTS

INTRODUCTION

I am grateful to God for the opportunity to write a book from my past experiences with a subject that tormented and devastated my life for many years. And, by the grace of God, what started as a mess, ended as a ministry!

Hence, it is my pleasure to write a book that addresses a global problem. It is a problem that is lurking in our homes, workplaces, neighborhoods, churches, personal life, professional life, political and spiritual life. It recognizes no age, color sex, race, belief, economic status, geographic location, success level, titles or lack thereof. It is the problem of "sexual immorality."

This moral epidemic continues to break record numbers, as the numbers soar with the growth of the human population.

Every person on the face of the earth faces sexual challenges, most people are affected by a sexual problem in one form or another. This is evidenced by the multiple billions of dollars being pumped into the sex industry. Our predominant interest in the things that include the word "sex"; sexual entertainment, sexual news, sexy people, sensuous songs, dance videos, and TV programs with sexual themes, and the list goes on.

However, this book is written from a Christian perspective to help the reader get a basic grip on the nature of sexual immorality by discussing the various shades, kinds, and types of sexual sin rampant in our world. Each sexual behavior is discussed by, defining, explaining, and advising. This book is not designed to be a cure-all, but to help give the reader a fundamental understanding on how to bring the sexual problem under control, and grasp of the "direction" that's needed to bring total healing and deliverance.

This book is not written to condemn the reader. It is written with the heart of God, showing God's love for you in spite of how far you've fallen! And the wisdom of God, showing that God and "only" God has the answer to your dilemma! For, it is the goal of the Holy Spirit to reach you, not destroy you!

This is a comprehensive book, written as a self-help reference tool, arranged in alphabetized format for quick reference, and personal devotion.

It is spiritual therapy with practical answers from the word of God.

Please, be advised, that many of the problems discussed in this book will require additional assistance through professional Christian counseling.

Above all, none of these principles, or advise, will produce any lasting results without a personal relationship with the Lord Jesus Christ.

ACKNOWLEDGMENTS

The Lord; thank you for inspiring my mind with your thoughts, anointing me to put your vision into a book, and entrusting me to carry this message to the nations.

My Church; to the greatest church in the world, thanks for standing by us and believing in us when we needed you the most.

My Children; Moriah, Shekirah, Jacob, Noah, Mecharlay, Joshua, Shekinah, Faith, Caleb, Louis and Marcella (daughter-in-law) and grandchildren (Nonte, Marcel, Tylan). You are my inspiration. And a special thanks to Noah for your great help in assisting with the image of the cover design.

Siblings; Arthur, Ronald, Deborah, Kenny, Rosalyn. God has been good to us. I thank God for wonderful brothers and sisters.

My Mother; you practically raised all six of us single-handedly, and did a marvelous job. Thank you for putting up with me from birth to adulthood . Allowing God to anoint you to watch over His investment! Love you Mom!

My Pastor; Bishop Keith A. Butler Sr.; thank you for encouraging me to put my ministry into a book.

Devon/Palmer Advertising; for your care and professional touch in this project.

Derrick Davie; for the motivation to write what you preach.

Dr. Elvira Hanley; for your spiritual encouragement.

Sabrina Black: for all of your motivation and availability. Thank you!

Ty Adams; to my wonderful and (full of surprises) sister in the Lord. Thank you for all your inspiration and technical support.

Family and Friends; thank you for all of your support.

Fellow-Pastors; thank you for your ministerial inspiration.

Dr. Myles Monroe; thank you for blessing this project with your global influence and thought provoking foreword.

Pastor Glen Plummer; for always being available to help my wife and I achieve maximum potential.

My beautiful wife; to the greatest woman I know! The mother of my children, and "love of my life." You are the "wind beneath my wings", giving me the strength to not come down from the altitudes of destiny, in spite of the winds of criticism and hostility. Thanks for saying yes, when the world said no! Love ya forever!

Abortion

Abortion- the act of ending a human life before birth. The reason I have listed this particular sin in a sexual context, was due to the undeniable fact that it is sadly, and generally the final result of sexual immorality. After the unwanted pregnancy, abortion is an attempt to make the problem go away, as if it never happened. According to the *"Online Encarta Encyclopedia",* approximately 46 million abortions are performed worldwide each year.

This breaks down to the deaths of approximately 127,000 babies a day, or 88 babies every minute, or two children every second. This is a staggering figure, considering the fact that contrary to popular belief, these babies are "human beings." I believe that one of the critical reasons for this atrocious act is "The Government." In 1973 our Supreme Court Justice System ruled in favor of "legalized abortion" over the infamous Roe vs .Wade case.

Throughout our history, massive destruction has always followed the legalization of sin. For example, when prayer was removed from our public schools, we lost our children to school dropouts, unwanted pregnancies, drugs, sex, gangs and the list goes on. Hence, it is no surprise that our teenage babies have gone from having babies to killing babies. We have created a murderous society.

To take the life of a human being brings destruction in many ways. But, I would like to briefly discuss what I believe are three of the most critical things that occur in an abortion. First, one destroys life, in *(Exodus 20:13)*, the scripture says *"You shall not murder."* Death affects a person on three levels: spirit, soul, and body. In *(1 Thessalonians 5:24)* the Bible teaches that every person consist of these three parts. Death results in the removal of a person's physical, spiritual, and soulish existence from the earth. At the point of death the Bible teaches that the spirit and soul is separated from the body and is no longer a part of life on earth. The body is put in a grave and the spirit and soul is either carried to God or sent to a place of judgment (hell; *Luke 16:19-31, James 2:26.*) Death ends the earthly existence of the spirit, soul and body. Thus, every murder that takes place destroys the human life on three levels." Second, one destroys peace, that is, your peace of mind. I often wondered which is worst, physical pain or mental pain. I learned over the years that physical pain is shorter, and much easier to cope with than mental pain. Memories of terrible experiences can remain in your thoughts for life. It is these types of traumatic experiences that can drive one into severe depression, leading to mental illness and a very chaotic life. However, it is the will of God that you have peace and soundness of mind (*Philippians 4:7, 2 Timothy 1:7.*) Thirdly, one destroys purpose, in *(Jeremiah 1:5,6 and Galatians 1:15)*, the scriptures teach that God is intimately involved in the human life long before birth. In *(Revelation 4:11)*, the scripture says, "everything (including people) was created for His pleasure." The unborn child was created for the pleasure of God. To abort an unborn is to destroy the pleasure of God. Divine pleasure is a part of God's purpose in creating man.

In *(Acts 13:36)*, the scripture teaches, *"after King David served his own generation by the will or plan of God, he fell asleep"* (or went to be with God.) Hallelujah. Every human being is born to fulfill a God ordained "service" to their generation. Thus, to destroy a child is to destroy a service that could have made a difference in that generation. Moreover, in *(Luke 1:44)*, the scriptures teach that babies have spiritual purpose and identity; "*the babe leaped in my womb for joy.*" Every born or unborn person is created to fulfill a divine service. We don't know who is in the womb of that mother contemplating abortion. There might be a pastor, and pastoral services that could have been provided for a lost and hurting church would be destroyed. There might be a president, and the presidential services that could have led a country out of its oppressive conditions would be destroyed. There might be a doctor, and the medical services that could have helped save so many lives, and perhaps the life of a dying member in your family, would be destroyed. We do not know who is in the womb. But, there's one thing we do know. There is a person, created with purpose. To destroy the person, would destroy the purpose. We have seen the unlimited destruction of abortion. If you are wrestling with the thought of abortion, there are other alternatives:

(a) your right to "informed consent" Informed consent is an agreement to receive a medical service after you have been thoroughly informed and have understood all the risks involved.

 (b) transference of custody—consider giving your child to a responsible family member, foster care agency or adoption agency. If you are trying to avoid abortion as a single, practice abstinence (*1 Thessalonians 4:3.*) If you are married, and do not desire to have children, use "contraceptives." God holds any parent responsible to properly and thoroughly raise a child. If you cannot provide proper care for a child for whatever reason, I urge you to *avoid pregnancy*. The God who wants us to be fruitful and have children, also wants us to "care" for them. (*Proverbs 22:5,6, Ephesians 6:4, 1 Timothy 5:8*)

(Advice)

Key Problem: If you are facing abortion; this is an issue of abuse and rejection. Most people who face the decision to abort a life have had an unfortunate history of abuse. This abuse has been mainly exhibited in the form of rejection. In most cases, they were either "abandoned" by their parents, parent-figures or "lost" them to death, and practically raised themselves. Subsequently, this life of rejection sends many into a tailspin of rejection after rejection. And because of a life of rejection, it is easy to, in turn, reject another life.

In *(Exodus 2:1-6)*, Moses was rejected as a baby. His mother felt she could no longer protect her child from the death decree ordered by the king, and abandoned Moses in an attempt to save him. Although, I understand this mother's actions, the bottom line was a "rejected" child. This is reflective of the many parents who face the same set of circumstances; the "helplessness" of raising a child. But Moses' story had a happy ending; God took a "reject" and made a "project." God raised up a broken life and led a broken people into a fulfilling future. Moses became one of the greatest leaders of one of the greatest nations of all times. Your life is not over. God is a *"Forgiver."* He will forgive you for everything that you've ever done (*1 John 1:9.*) He is a *"Provider" (Psalm 23:1.*) He can take care of you and your baby. Yield to God and let Him take your broken past and make a great future.

To overcome abortion, pray, and ask God to help you apply the following steps:

1. Repent-Turn away from this sin, ask God to forgive you. *(Acts 3:19)*

2. Consider your options (adoption agency, foster care, family members, keep your baby)

3. Parenting Classes- *(Proverbs 22:5,6)*

4. Counsel- Seek professional counseling. *(Proverbs 11:14)*

5. Church- Join a Bible teaching/living church. Let God nurture the social void, through spiritual parents (pastors) *(1 Corinthians 4:15, Ephesians 4:11,12)*

6. Ministry Groups- Join a mens'/womens' fellowship. Let God build self-worth through caring relationships. *(Hebrews 10:25)*

7. Word Study- Take a Bible and a *Strong's Concordance*, look up as many references as you can on life and love (God's.)

For additional help and information See *Fornication.*

Abuse

Abuse- the act of presenting sexual behavior in a manner that misuses, or violates one's rights. Sexual abuse covers such a broad range of sexual activity that my focus is to cover the nature of sexual abuse, versus the individual types. However, remember sexual abuse always includes a violation of someone's rights and/ or decisions. Examples, would be rape, incest, pedophilia, even prostitution and pornography, where the sexual workers are treated as objects. Where does this type of abuse come from? I believe it comes from two primary factors: First, this abuse starts with a "seed." Any person who has ever been sexually abused or person who has sexually abused someone, had a beginning. There was a first time somewhere in the life of the victim. This abusive experience was the planting of a seed. Harm was making its mark on their life. In *(Galatian 6:7)*, the scripture says, *"for whatsoever a man sows that he will also reap."*

When a person suffers harm, it is a sowing of pain into their total being. Harm goes in and can destroy on all levels: mental, emotional, spiritual, verbal, physical, social, financial and so on. The intensity of the abuse determines the depth of damage. Sexual abuse delivers incredible harm; it is a two-edged sword that destroys both the abuser and the victim at the same time. It is a robber that takes dignity and self-worth from the victim, and love and ability to respect the values of others from the abuser. Both the victim and the abuser are left with damage.

In *(Genesis 16:1-15)*, the scriptures record the story of Sarai (Sarah) who is infertile and cannot bear children, becoming a victim of abuse after she willingly asks her husband to have sexual intercourse with Hagar (the concubine; slave-wife.) After Hagar conceives and bears a child (Ishmael), Sarai feels "violated." Behind being abused, she goes from the abused to the abuser; verse 6 of this chapter says "and when Sarai dealt hardly (harsh) with her, she fled from her presence." The term "hardly" means to abuse. Sarah's (Sarai) abusiveness started with the seed of "being abused."

Second, abuse is fostered by an "environment." The environment of our communities is filled with things that feed abusive behavior. Things like billboards advertising sexual pictures or messages, pornography, magazines, peep shows, prostitution, seductive dance videos, negative television programs, failed marriages, dysfunctional families, abuse of authority; these and other factors helped shape an abusive mentality and have in some cases led to mental illness *(1 Corinthians 15:33.)*

One must choose to become the environment or change the environment. This was the scenario with Paul and Silas in *(Acts 16:25-31)*, after being placed in prison, they turned to God in "prayer and Praise," and God turned the *"jail house into a church house."* They had to choose whether to "breakdown" or "breakout." What are you doing with your environment? Remember, environments can carry deadly potential.

For the sake of identifying abuse, I would like to share some general signs. The following is a list compiled from "*A Betrayal of Innocence*" by David B. Peters and "*When Child Abuse Comes to Church*" by Bill Anderson.

Behavioral Indicators of Sexual Abuse in Infants, Preschoolers and Older Children:

1. Uneasiness around previously trusted persons

2. Sexualized behavior (excessive masturbation, sexually inserting objects, explicit sex play with other children)

3. Fear of rest rooms, showers or baths

4. Fear of being alone with the opposite sex

5. Nightmares on a regular basis or about the same person

6. Abrupt personality changes

7. Uncharacteristic hyperactivity

8. Moodiness or excessive crying

9. Aggressive or violent behavior toward other children

10. Unusual need for assurance of love

11. Passive or withdrawn behavior

12. Specific knowledge of sexual facts and terminology beyond developmental age

13. Wearing multiple layers of clothing to bed; or wetting of bed after being broken of that problem

14. Acting like a parent (parentified behavior)

15. Attempts to make him or herself undesirable

16. Eating disorders

17. Tendency to seek out or totally avoid adults

18. Frequent tardiness or absence from school, especially if the teacher is male

19. Toys or money acquired with no explanation

20. Self-conscious behavior, especially of the body

Behavior Indicators of Sexual Abuse in Adults:

1. Sexual difficulties (usually regarding intimacy issues)

2. Distrust of the opposite sex

3. Inappropriate choice of partners

4. Multiple marriages

5. Extreme dependence upon or anger toward a parent

6. Progressive breakdown of communication and eventual emotional detachment from children

7. Sexual promiscuity

8. Drug or alcohol abuse

9. Extremely low self-esteem

10. Nightmares or flashbacks

11. Continual victimization (seemingly unable to assert or protect one's self)

12. Eating disorder

13. May see self-worth only in sexuality

14. Self-punishing behaviors

15. Homosexual orientation

16. Body shame

(ADVICE)

Key Problem: If you are facing abuse as the abused or the abuser; this is an issue with abuse and nurture. A life of abuse comes out of abuse itself, and failure to grow in a healthy environment.

To overcome abuse; pray, and ask God to help you apply the following steps:

(a) Healing- You will need healing of your mind, emotions and will. But, you must also understand that "only" God can heal a broken heart. *(Isaiah 61:1)*

(b) Honesty- You must not deny that you may be struggling with abuse issues. This can continue to hinder the overall growth of your life, and hold up your God ordained destiny. You must be willing to "acknowledge" your true feelings and weaknesses. You must be willing to deal with the "I" in your pain: I have a problem, I am struggling, I need help. Don't live in denial. Get honest with yourself and acknowledge that something is wrong. *(1 John 1:9,10, Luke 15:18,21)*

(c) Desire- After you acknowledge that there is a problem, you must "desire" to act on the solution. For example, if a patient does not desire to be healed, a doctor is hopeless. Jesus taught the importance of desire in *(St. John 5:5,6.)*

(d) Time- Your recovery will require God taking you through an inner and outer process of restoration. This will take "time." This process will include improvements, and failures, growth and setbacks, ups and downs, but, be patient. The rewards are worth it all. *(James 1:4, Psalm 23:3)*

(e) Forgive- This term literally means to "pardon" or "release."

There are at least three people you must forgive:

The person who wronged you. Yourself, some people blame themselves, and struggle with releasing themselves from the past. God, some people blame God, and feel that if God had been there, they would have never got hurt. It is important to release anyone who you feel has ever hurt you. Unforgiveness can lead to "torment" *(Matthew 18:21-35.)* God can help heal your "memories" *(Isaiah 54:4.)* Release them from being held guilty. Forgive. *(Matthew 6:12, Mark 11:24, Genesis 3:12)*

(f) Pain- Pain is not always destructive. The Lord gave me the illustration of a "cut hand." The moment you are cut, there is a throbbing or pain in the place of injury, because the blood is "rushing" to the area to aid in healing the hand. In actuality, pain is apart of the process used to heal the hand. Recovery is painful because you have to forgive those who hurt you, face the truth, and be patient with things you don't want to deal with. Hurting is normal, and God can use it to repair your heart and rebuild your mind. *(1 Peter 5:9,10)*

(g) Trust- You must learn to open up, and depend upon trustworthy help. You must learn to trust God; *(Proverbs 3:5,6)* *"He will never leave you nor forsake you"*, and you must begin trusting "people." God will send people whom the Holy Spirit will use to help you recover. *(Luke 5:17-20)*

(h) Love- You must learn to love God and love people. It is easy to harbor anger, and hatred behind an injury. Recovery involves learning to love. *(Matthew 22:37-39, 1 Peter 4:8.)*

(i) positive confessions—speak to yourself everyday, the things that God promised you in the word of the Lord"

Addiction

Addiction- an uncontrollable habit. There are at least five major addictions in the human race: food, gambling, drugs, alcohol, and sex. Sexual addiction is by far the worst addiction that a person can face. The reason being, man is a sex-being. Sex is part of man's nature, and make up. Sexual addiction, and signs of addiction are not limited to the male gender. But this practice is widely spreading among the female population, who are referred to as "nymphomaniacs."

Even though man must have food to live, in general he expresses a much greater desire for sexual pleasure. In *(Genesis 1:28)*, the scriptures teach, that God told Adam and Eve to *"be fruitful and multiply."* Adam and Eve were to multiply themselves or produce more people. The only way to produce more people, is through sexual intercourse. This meant that God made man with sexual ability. Folks, this is where the sex-drive came from—God. Never, and I say "never" ask God to take away your sex-drive, because you feel helplessly out of control. Pray for domination, not elimination of your libido (drive.)

The experience that God called a blessing, *"and He blessed them, and said be fruitful [sex], and multiply* (Genesis 1:28)*,* was perverted by the devil. Subsequently, sex was taken out of its context (marriage), leaving at least half the world, in a state of sexual addiction.

I am convinced that millions of people are addicted to sex and don't even know it. That's not hard to believe, when you look at the alarming rate of divorces stemming from adultery. The incredible growth spread of AIDS and sexually transmitted diseases. There are the gruesome cases of abortion's climbing rate, coming from unwanted pregnancies produced out of wedlock—not to mention the billions of dollars that are channeled annually into the sex industry. These reports clearly point to a worldwide problem with sexual addiction. According to Dr. Patrick Carnes, in "Don't Call It Love, Recovery From Sexual Addiction" he states the following signs of sexual addiction:

1. A pattern of out-of-control behavior
2. Severe consequences due to sexual behavior
3. Inability to stop despite adverse consequences
4. Persistent pursuit of self-destructive or high-risk behavior
5. Ongoing desire or effort to limit sexual behavior
6. Sexual obsession and fantasy as a primary coping strategy
7. Increasing amounts of sexual experience because the current level of activity is no longer sufficient
8. Severe mood changes around sexual activity
9. Inordinate amounts of time spent in obtaining sex, being sexual, or recovering from sexual experience
10. Neglect of important social, occupational, or recreational activity because of sexual behavior.

For most of my life, beginning with my adolescent years "I" was addicted to sex. This unrestrained craving, that the Bible calls lasciviousness, the Greek word being "aselgeia" pronounced (as-elg-i-a) was steering my life into one perversion after another (*Ephesians 4:19.*) This continued into my adult life, and into my Christian life, and into my life as a church leader. (To hear my personal testimony on sexual addiction, consult your local bookstores for my two-tape series entitled: *"Sampson and Delilah"*)

One day in the middle of my aftermath of sexual ruin, I looked at my entire life, my family, my church, and my friends. The church-world, where I was well-known and respected as a minister, my joy, my peace of mind, my future, was literally going down the drain before my eyes. In the "darkest" hour of my life, God came to me, and spoke light. (*St. John 8:12.*) The very words of God flooded my soul with understanding. For the first time, I saw sexual sin in its true nature. An endless journey of life-sucking pleasure (*Proverbs 6:32,33, 7:21-27.*) Sex had become an idol. God had to help me give up my sex-god (*Exodus 20:3.*) I didn't realize how much I depended on sex, until God challenged me with truth. An idol is anything that is giving supreme or highest recognition. This is the very reason an idol is also called a "god." I truly gave sex more recognition than I gave God. When I was lonely, I turned to sex. When I was angry, I turned to sex. When I needed comfort, I turned to sex. These were things that I should have taken to God, in total trust. I remember God speaking these simple words "*I am.*" God reassured me with His word (*Exodus 3:14*) by saying "*I am.*" Whatever I needed. Whatever I was trying to find, "*I am*" says the Lord.

I repented (turned away) from my sexual addiction. And God restored "everything" I lost, and has increased my life with indescribable success. My wife and I are happy, at peace, and living very well. My church has grown almost ten times in size. We have recently purchased a new church. We are holding two Sunday morning services, preparing for three. We host a very popular Christian TV, and Radio Talk show, and God has given us amazing success in the local bookstores with our ministry products. There is no limit, to what God will do, for any person who will "totally" turn their heart over to will of God (*Deuteronomy 28:1-14.*)

Believe it or not, the body can be "trained" to obey your heart. *(Hebrews 5:14)* says " *But strong meat belongs to them that are of full age even those who by reason of use have their senses exercised to discern both good and evil.*" The word "*senses*" refer to the perceptions and functions of the body. In other words you can condition your body to reject and become uncomfortable with sexual sin.

However, this success did not come overnight, but through some simple, yet powerful steps, God led me to where I am today. Those steps were: prayer, Bible study, fasting, obedience, fellowship and service. This is not an attempt to exhaust the list of things that should be included in a restoration process: counseling, accountability, etc.

Due to the limitation of time, purpose and space, I want to focus on the core of sexual addiction. Remember, addiction is a pattern. God spoke to me and revealed the most basic things that are needed to overcome "addiction." The Lord said I needed a spiritual pattern, to replace my sexual pattern. The Bible supports this "key" point, in *(Galatians 5:16)* saying, *"if we walk in the Spirit, we will not fulfill the lust of the flesh."* The focus is on the word walk. Walk is a very important word in the New Testament. This word indicates living, flowing, or continuing in the power of the Holy Spirit.

Now, let's return to the idea of a pattern. A pattern is simply a continuation of activities. Now, I understood that the key to sexual victory, was learning to walk or continue in the power of the Holy Spirit. But, I was only half way to the finish line. I knew I had to continue in the Holy Spirit, but how? This is where God revealed those six basic steps (patterns) to victory, that I previously mentioned.

Now, I want to change the language from "steps, walking, and patterns" to schedule. All of these terms are synonymous with the word, schedule. A schedule is a pattern or continuation of events, set to happen at a given time. This is the word I really want to talk to you about. The other synonyms were used to bring more clarity to the importance of this word "schedule."

The Lord placed me on a basic schedule that consisted of the following steps:

1. Prayer- Learning to schedule daily time to talk with God (*Matthew 26: 39-41, Mark 1:35, 1 John 5:14.*)

2. Bible study- Learning to schedule daily time to examine, and search the word of God. *(2 Timothy 2:15, 1 Peter 2:2, Psalm 1:2,3)*

3. Fasting- Learning to abstain from food, and/or water to receive from God. I suggest a minimum fast of 3 days (36 hours) or more, and maintenance fasting of at least 1 day (24 hours) a week. Most people have to build up by starting with a partial fast (*Daniel 10:3.*)

Remember, sexual sin is a deeper problem, requiring a deeper approach, and a deeper anointing (*Matthew 17:21.*) Fasting will help put sexual passion back to sleep (*Song of Solomon 3:7.*)

4. Obedience- Learning to hear, and immediately do the word of God. *(James 1:22, Matthew 4:1-11)*

5. Fellowship- Learning to commit to the sharing, and partaking of a personal relationship and intimacy with God, a local church and its relationships, church affiliations, and spiritual rehabilitation programs. *(1 John 1:3, Hebrews 10:25, 13:7,17, Acts 2:41-47)*

6. Service- Learning to stay occupied with spiritual work. Getting involved in a local church, or volunteering community services. If you have struggled with this problem, remember your life was occupied with "serving" the devil. Get busy for Jesus. God honors faithful service. *(Matthew 25:23)*

Important: the amount of time that one should spend with God, will vary according to the person. However, a safe guide to determine needed time with God, is to seek God long enough to see growth, or changes in your life. If you are suffering from sexual addiction, I recommend that you take these steps under spiritual guidance. Seek spiritual counsel and enter a sexual help program. Remember, any help that you seek must evolve around these six spiritual steps. Maintaining a spiritual schedule of the six steps, will eliminate addictive patterns and habits of the flesh.

(ADVICE)

Key Problem: If you are facing sexual addiction, this is an issue with patterns and self-control. To overcome sexual addiction; pray, and ask God to help you apply the six steps mentioned above.

Adultery

Adultery- the act of sex between two people, who are not married to one another. In (*Exodus 20:14*), the Hebrew word for adultery is "naaph" pronounced (naw-af) which means sex with the wife or betrothed of another. Before I proceed, I want to point out a very significant word that we must understand to appreciate the institution of marriage. The word "betrothed" means "engaged" to be married. In the Jewish history, when a man and woman became engaged it was so serious, that the man and woman were called husband and wife, even before marriage. (*Matthew 1:18,19.*)

In the Western culture, engagement is treated loosely and lightly. But, it is important to note that marriage is so important to God, that when two people purpose to get engaged, although they are not husband and wife, God treats the period of engagement just as serious, as if they were husband and wife. Anything connected to marriage, God takes it seriously.

In (*Matthew 5:28*), Jesus said *"but I say to you that whoever looks at a woman to lust for her has already committed adultery with her in his heart."*

These previous passages tell us that adultery can occur physically and mentally. And, although the physical act of adultery throughout scripture carried the more serious judgment, the mental act of adultery is serious to God. It revealed that two people can yet be together without ever touching or being in one another's presence.

Nevertheless, because adultery or infidelity is such a very complex subject, I will only seek to discuss the basic facets of adultery, to help provide a fundamental grasp on such an alarmingly perplexed issue. Adultery is one of the leading causes of divorce. Marriage experts agree that one out of every two marriages will end in divorce. Which says, according to the current trend, married couples have only a 50% chance of surviving. And without God, this is very true. Nevertheless, I want to continue talking to you about the nature of adultery. What is it? It is a death blow to the marital covenant. In *(Malachi 2:15,16)*, the Bible calls marriage a covenant or agreement.

When a couple performs wedding vows, they are making a lifetime agreement to be with one another. But, adultery destroys the agreement. It goes against everything you agreed to stand for. Nevertheless, the destructive nature of infidelity cannot be described by words. Its destruction is beyond a true description. Allow me to present some scriptural illustrations to help you gather some grasp of the seriousness of adultery. In *(Leviticus 20:10)*, the Bible says *"The man who commits adultery with another man's wife, he who commits adultery with his neighbor's wife, the adulterer and the adulteress shall surely be put to death."*

In the Old Testament the judgment for adultery was the "death penalty." Such serious punishment reflected the serious nature of adultery. God revealed to me, that the depth of human pain behind an adulterous affair is so great that under the Old Testament, God had the adulterers put to death. They were permanently removed. This revealed how serious and dangerous adultery is to both the marriage covenant and the human heart. In *(2 Samuel 16:20-22, 20:3)*, the Bible records how King David was violated by his son (*Absalom*) who had sexual intercourse with David's ten concubines (slave-wives) in an effort to revolt against the throne of David. When King David discovered the infidelity with his concubines, the pain was so deep that the Bible says *"He did not go in to them"*—that is, David did not have sex with his concubines for the rest of their life. Can you imagine that? The damage of adultery was so great that he never touched (sexually) his wives ever again. Moreover, *(Job 31:9-12)* states that adultery is a *"fire."* And the obvious meaning is that "like fire" adultery destroys and causes great ruin. If you have ever followed sex crimes, some of the greatest "crimes of passion" have followed the discovery of an affair.

Infidelity can rip a heart, and snap a mind. An affair has the potential to transform a "happy home" into a "hell home." It can convert the once sweetest person in the world into a walking time bomb. As I said earlier, adultery is serious business.

Another word for adultery, is unfaithfulness. And unfaithfulness is made up of two primary aspects: unfaithfulness outside of the marriage, and unfaithfulness inside the marriage. One, can be unfaithful to the marital covenant without ever involving a "third party." All affairs start from the unfaithfulness that occurs inside of the marriage, first.

We put a lot of emphasis on the cheating that occurs outside of the marriage. However, allow me to challenge this traditional position, by defining the term "unfaithful." This word means to be disloyal or untrue. Untrue to What? Untrue to the wedding vows. The vows were promises and agreements to fulfill every marital responsibility to the fullest. In *(Ephesians 5:22-25)*, the Bible teaches that one of the primary roles of a woman in a marriage is "submission" and one of the primary roles of a man in the marriage is to "love." Each of these roles are divine duties, and with duties come responsibilities. Therefore, when a man or a woman fail within their marriage to carry out their God-given duties they are being unfaithful or untrue to the responsibilities of the marital covenant.

Ironically, many marriages are ending without the involvement of a third party, due to marital neglect or unfaithfulness. Nevertheless, it is upon this very premise that marriages become easy targets to adultery. Which brings us to the infamous question; why do people cheat? Without question it is embedded within the ground of an "unfaithful heart." And before I continue, please understand that adultery is always unfaithfulness, but unfaithfulness is not always adultery. However, it is the heart that begins to neglect commitment to the responsibilities of the marriage, that become extremely vulnerable to an adulterous affair. Adultery is an act of going outside of the marriage, whether mentally or physically, for sexual fulfillment. It is one's search or quest for something that they fill is lacking. And I want to be clear on this point; infidelity does not always occur because the victim of infidelity did something wrong. But, many times an affair occurs because something was already wrong with the spouse who committed the affair.

Often times people enter relationships with unresolved pain. And because of many issues that have been repressed and overlooked; a person can find themselves going from one relationship to another, never finding peace and happiness until they find Jesus Christ. (*St. John 4.*) A person's lack and cause for adultery could be their own brokenness. Nonetheless, the atmosphere for infidelity is often created by the lack of fulfillment from a persons emotional needs. Emotional needs are about feeling good. Things that make you feel good, is the very center of a healthy relationship.

Emotional needs is the arena that determines if the marriage is going to succeed or fail. If you focus on this area, and discover what makes your spouse happy, and commit to nourish those needs; you will have a marriage that is hard for outsiders to get in. But, if you neglect the things that make your spouse feel good; adultery is almost inevitable. (*1 Corinthians 7:5.*)

One of the most common areas of neglect is sex. For example, some women are sexually withdrawn from their husbands. Sometimes the reason is abuse, which I'll address later, but another unspoken reason is the lack of sexual education. There are many women who were told to abstain from sex, but never taught about sex their entire life. And when they get married, because all they've known is the danger of sex, but not the beauty that God has created for the marriage-bed; they are practically nonfunctional, afraid, shy, and live in a false sense of being violated.

Nevertheless, some of the most common reasons for affairs are: loneliness, abuse, lack of attention, disrespect, anger, insensitivity, poor communication and lying. Marriage experts agree that these reasons are far more serious than lack of money, lack of sex, overweight or underweight, unattractive appearance, or the lack of lavish activities. Adultery thrives off of the neglect of "inner needs", not material provision and physical success. Many will give their spouse the world, but fail to give themselves. However, there are also signs to the presence of adultery.

What are some common signs of cheating? The following are generally sure signs:

(1)   Decrease in sex

(2)   Less communication

(3)   Changes in physical appearance (new hair style, new dress style, sudden interest in physical fitness)

(4) Changes in spending habits

(5) Changes in behavior around the opposite sex

(6) Sexual scents in the clothes

(7) Suddenly missing in action a lot

(8) Suddenly arriving home late on a regular basis

(9) Caught in circumstances without an explanation

(10) Female or male things found in the car

(11) A need for private communication (new pager, cell phone, can't talk in front of spouse)

One or more of these signs could be evidence of the presence of adultery in the marriage. However, when adultery is discovered, it releases a cycle of pain: anger, hurt, disbelief (shock), denial, blame and hopelessness. The spouse who has become a victim to an affair will go through these feelings accompanied with mood swings. Easily, shifting from laughter into uncontrollable crying, from a good moment to a terrible day, or month, or year. Infidelity causes the heart to become fragile, and unbearably sensitive. It doesn't take much to get a victim of adultery unraveled and completely shutdown.

This cycle of feelings will happen repeatedly until the victim-spouse enters the stage of inner healing. Moreover, the cheating spouse may ironically, go through a phase of withdrawal. If the cheating-spouse became attached to the third party, the cheating-spouse may feel that being challenged to separate from their lover, was an act of robbery.

What became valuable was taken away. The cheating-spouse will feel anger, depression, anxiety, and anti-sociable. Infidelity strikes both spouses resulting in major damage.

When you discover infidelity, how do you approach it?

In *(Hosea 2:1-16)*, the Bible records the renown story of Hosea and Gomer. Hosea was a prophet of God, and Gomer was his adulterous wife. This story has a twofold application; first, it literally speaks of the love that God teaches Hosea for his promiscuous wife, and second, this love is used to illustrate God's infinite love for His people (Israel.) Because of this two-fold purpose, this chapter gives us some very helpful strategies for coping with infidelity.

The strategies are as follows:

(1) Confrontation- An affair must be approached. You cannot be reserved, and figure it will work itself out. (v2.)

(2) Separation- You must demand that the cheating-spouse ends the affair immediately. (v2.)

(3) Honesty- An affair must be brought to the open. It is important to "expose" the affair, and be as truthful as you can. Remember, the power of an affair is in its secretive nature. It is powerful, because of what one does not know *(Hosea 4:6.)* When light or honesty is brought to the situation it exposes the secrets held in the dark. Light weakens the presence of darkness. This means that an open life destroys the strength of secrets *(St. John 3:19,20.)*

(4) Aggression- An affair must be strongly approached. This matter must be treated with drive and intensity (v2.)

(5) Suspension- Failure to live out marital responsibilities eliminates the rights to marital privileges. One must prayerfully, ask God what to withhold or take from their spouse during the course and aftermath of the affair. For example, this could mean no sex, dating, a separation, etc. (vv 2,12.)

(6) Intervention- If a marriage is to recover from an affair, the abused spouse must get involved. Eliminate any and all opportunities for the affair to continue. For example, you would not encourage your spouse to take a second job in the name of saving the marriage, spending more time away from home, and less time with you, or allowing your spouse to work out an affair without your involvement. You would have every right to stand up and block all attempts to continue the affair (vv 6,7.)

(7) Love - None of these strategies will work without the right attitude. The affair has to be approach in love. Your aim must be to save the marriage, not destroy it (vv 14-16, *Jeremiah 31:3.*)

(8) Pray- This is the single strategy that gives power to all the strategies. One of the greatest threats to an affair, is a spouse who knows how to intercede (pray.) Often time the atmosphere is so intense that both spouses cannot talk with one another. But, when you learn how to "pray the word", pinpoint your prayers and pray the will of God; God can strengthen the praying spouse, and bring conviction and deliverance upon the wayward spouse. Prayer brings deliverance. (Acts *12:5-8.*)

It is important to note that a marriage cannot even begin to heal, until an affair has ended. However, once the affair ends, this is just the beginning of marital recovery. The affair has left major damage.

So, how do you recover from an affair? The following steps will be very helpful.

(1) Repent- The first critical step in destroying an affair and its consequences, is for the cheating-spouse to acknowledge and "turn" from the affair. *(Acts 3:19, 2 Samuel 12:13)*

(2) Healing- An affair causes damage in both spouses, resulting in the need for inner healing. For example, if a person has a nail pierced through their hand, the source of pain would be the "nail",

and upon removing the nail, you would have removed the source of the problem. However, you would still have a hole in your hand. The point in this illustration, is that removing the sin from a person's life is only the first step, but the consequences of the hole will require a period of healing. *(Isaiah 61:1)*

(3) Time- The damage behind an affair is so extensive that a "quick fix" solution is not a likely occurrence. Prepare for what could be a long process of change (mood swings, highs and lows, good days and bad days.) Unfortunately, one of the very vital areas of the marriage that becomes affected by the vicious aftermath of infidelity is the sex life. In most cases it dies. It affects the center of sexual life, the mind. This is an abuse that affects the mind with unlimited depth. Sometimes a spouse will substitute this void with pornography and masturbation, which causes further damage to the mind. The sex life can only revive, by changing the victim's mind. The victim-spouse will have to have the mental pictures of failure, replaced by the "experiences of success."

Hence, the cheating-spouse must be consistent with applying the word of God, and doing the right thing. (Romans *12:1,2.*) To force sex on your spouse under conditions of abuse, is "forced sex" which is equivalent to rape. It is always the will of God for a husband and wife to apply both the "mind" and body during sex. *(1Corinthians 7:3,4.)* Remember, *(Proverbs 6:33)*, adultery delivers a wound or blow to the marriage. This results in a spouse who is now broken and fragmented. Which explains why it is difficult for the victim-spouse to give of themselves; there's not much of them left.

(4) Restitution- An affair robs the marriage. The cheating-spouse is now in debt to the victim-spouse, and the focus should be on how to repay their spouse for what the affair took from the marriage: trust, respect, interest, security, unity, etc. *(Exodus 22:1-3)*

(5) Forgive- The focus of the victim-spouse must be to forgive or release the cheating-spouse from guilt and blame, in order for the marriage to began the process of healing. Due to the grave challenge and difficulty with the forgiveness of an affair; the question often arises, how? Let's consider the following steps:

(a) Forgiveness is the will of God- biblical forgiveness is unconditional. This type of forgiveness is expressed regardless of the offender's actions. *(Mark 11:25, Matthew 18:21,22)*

(b) God forgave man- when Jesus died for the sins of the world, God was providing the "ground" on which He could legally forgive man. Because God forgave, He has a right to ask man to forgive.

(c) Ask God to heal your heart- an affair leaves tremendous pain in the thoughts, and emotions. *(Isaiah 61:1)*

(d) Understand that God will repay you- an offender may never apologize or make good behind such a disastrous decision. It is God who will reward you for your lost. *(Isaiah 49:2)*

(e) Avoid dwelling on the past- don't spend too much time thinking and focusing on the affair itself. God can heal your "thoughts." *(Isaiah 54:4,5 Philippians 4:8)*

(f) Don't continue talking about the affair- Your words can trap your life in a bondage of misery *(Proverbs 6:2.)* God will permit a season of pain *(Ecclesiastes 3:4)* but at some point God desires to move you past your pain into your purpose. *(Psalm 30:5)*

(g) Approach your abuser- It is helpful for both the victim and the abuser to expose the sin, by letting the abuser know that they have offended you. *(Matthew 5:23-26)*

(h) Say aloud, that you forgive the people who injured you. Confession helps bring healing. *(James 5:16)*

(i) Start a new lifestyle- It is important for the victim to start living again. Set new goals and plans, which will help you look to an exciting future, while taking your mind off of a miserable past. *(Colossians 3:2, Romans 6:4)*

6. Pain- Pain can be destructive or constructive. All pain is not bad. God can use pain to heal. For example, if you have ever been cut anywhere on the body, the pain creates a throbbing feeling. But, the throbbing pain is actually the blood rushing to the injured area to cause healing. What we have is, pain being used to heal. An affair hurts. It hurts to talk about it, deal with it, wait in it, and etc. But, God will use this pain to strengthen you and restore you. *(1 Peter 5:10, 2 Corinthians 4:17)*

7. Trust- An affair destroys trust. It is important to reach out and learn to trust again. God will send people who will help you rebuild your life and restore trust. Join a Bible teaching/living church to receive spiritual nourishment and comfort. *(Hebrews 10:25, Luke 4: 18-25, James 5:16)*

8. Love- An affair can destroy the ability to love. Love is key to the healing process. Open your heart and God will teach you how to love again. (*Galatians 6:5, 1 Peter 4:8, Matthew 22:37-40*)

Adultery robs the marriage of everything that God intended a couple to enjoy, but God is into restoration. He can put back everything the marriage ever lost.

(ADVICE)

Key Problem: If you are struggling with adultery; this is an issue of loyalty and nurture. The relationship lacks the ability to be true to the responsibilities of marriage. Most people who commit adultery were deprived of the opportunity to be nourished by strong relationships. And subsequently, never learned how to have a healthy relationship.

The foundation to a healthy relationship is lots of "giving" (hugs, kisses, touching, communication, lovemaking, dating, gifts, respect etc.) The healthiest marriages are relationships, where each spouse gives abundantly.

into the marriage on a daily basis. The principle of giving in *(Luke 6:38)*, teaches us that giving will cause giving in your spouse.

I want to present some vital areas, where giving will help build loyalty, and thus, help proof the marriage against adultery.

First, I want to list five important areas of negative giving. Dr. Willard F. Harley Jr. in his book, *"Love Busters"* states the following areas:

(a) Angry Outbursts- Releasing uncontrolled anger against you spouse.

(b) Disrespectful Judgments- Making decisions that do not consider the opinions and values of the other spouse.

(c) Annoying Behavior- Doing things that irritate and upset your spouse.

(d) Selfish Demands- Asking your spouse to do something that only benefits you.

(e) Dishonesty- Lying and hiding the truth from your spouse.

These are five major areas that will quickly deteriorate the foundation of a marriage.

However, there are six areas that require much "giving" to build loyalty:

(1) Verbal- A strong relationship consist of good communication. (*Song of Solomon 1,2,4 chpts. Ephesians 4:29*)

(2) Mental- It is important to share your thoughts, plans, goals, and basically have a mutual perspective on life. (*Amos 3:3*)

(3) Physical- Make sure that you keep your body looking attractive to your spouse. (exercise, groom, hygiene) (*Song of Solomon 1, 2,4,5 chpts.*)

(4) Emotional- The feelings of each spouse must become important. Remember, a relationship is most stable when two people are "happy." (1 Corinthians *7:3,4, Ephesians 5:28,29, Song of Solomon 1,2,4*)

(5) Social- Don't allow the fun and spice to vanish from your marriage. It is important to do things together (trips, games, sports, pillow fights, surprise ventures, etc.) Don't rust out, live out God's best for your life. (*Proverbs 17:22*)

(6) Spiritual- God must be the center of your marriage. Above being husband and wife, you are spiritual partners in the Gospel. (*Matthew 6:33, 1 Peter 3:1*)

In conclusion, hang around couples with strong marriages. They are "givers", and believe in lots of nourishment.

Remember., God is a giver, and He gives to us all the time. Model your marriage after God, and you'll never go wrong. (*Ephesians 5:22-33*)

For additional help and information See *Fornication.*

Anal Sex

Anal Sex- the act of using the anus (bottom-hole) for sexual pleasure. Contrary to popular belief, this practice is not limited to homosexuals. It is also, practiced widely among heterosexuals (opposite sexes) males, and females, single, or married. Interestingly, anal sex has been used by many as a form of birth control. An opportunity to have sex, and avoid pregnancy. Some, have practiced this form of sex to avoid the lost of virginity. Nevertheless, even a virgin can be sexually defiled by dishonoring her body and perverting her thoughts (*Matthew 5:28, Romans 12:1.*)

Anal sex has also been called sodomy. The word sodomy comes from the homosexual, and anal activity practiced by the men of the City of Sodom (*Genesis 19:1-11.*) Anal sex goes against the nature of the human body. God created the anus (bottom-hole) to excrete, and rid the body of its waste. This opening was never created for pleasure, but for waste. To use the anus for any other purpose, goes against nature, or is unnatural.

In (*Romans 1:27*), the scriptures teach that this group of people were committing sexual acts that were unnatural. These acts against the natural use were prohibited by God. Moreover, in (*Romans 1:26*), the Bible uses the words "vile affections." This term comes from the Greek words 'atimia" pronounced (at-ee-mee-ah) and pathos pronounced (path-os) which refers to sexual activity that dishonors a person.

Anal sex is both unnatural, and dishonorable. Medically, it is a proven fact that the tissue of the anus is very delicate, and hence, easily subject to damage and infection. People who have sought to engage in anal sex , generally use heavy lubrication, as if the penis was not naturally designed to fit.

Dr. Hilda Hutcherson, a gynecologist, says, in her book *"What Your Mother Never Told You About Sex"* ... *"to prevent vaginal infections you should not move a finger, penis or toy from your anus to your vagina without washing first."*

It appears that even the differences of the bacteria that is in the vagina and in the anus, says that God did not intend for the two to mix. To take the penis from the anus to the vagina is an unnatural mix. I believe that this unnatural order tells us that God never intended for the anus to be apart of the sexual experience.

The physical order of creation, says a lot about the wisdom of God . You don't want to go against nature's order. It is rebellion towards God (*Romans 1:20.*)

(ADVICE)

Key Problem: If you are struggling with anal sex, this is an issue with unnatural affections and honor.

To overcome anal sex, pray, and ask God to help you apply the following steps: See key problem, under Fornication.

Bestiality

Bestiality- the act of a person engaging in sexual activity with an animal. This act is also referred to as zoophilia. Sex between animals and people has been explored for years. Certain animals have been more commonly targeted in bestiality such as: the cow, horse, dog, cat, birds, snakes, monkey, and sheep. Other animals such as the lion, zebra, leopard, dog and giraffe has been specially noted, as being trainable for performing sex acts with humans. Although, some have desired animals to the extent of trying to crossbreed, or mate with an animal, there is no record of an animal producing a human offspring, or record of a human producing an animal. In one bizarre incident, it was noted that a Denver cowboy requested a license to marry his horse, of course he was denied.

Nevertheless, In (*Leviticus 18:23*), the scripture says *"that man should not have sex with a beast."* There is no record of an animal produces a human offspring, or record of a human producing an animal. The simple reason being, God did not design man to have sex with an animal. Did you know, out of all the species that God created, only man has the ability to have sex face to face?

If you have ever observed animals mating with one another it has generally been from the back or sometimes the side, depending upon the species. This privilege speaks to the level of intimacy that God created for people with people, not people with beast.

In *(Genesis 2:18)* the word "helpmeet" comes from the Hebrew term "ezer" pronounced (ay-zer) which means, helper, and counterpart. A counterpart is a part similar to another part. It can do exactly what the other part can do. It can counter or return activity for activity. Adam was alone with the animals, before Eve (counterpart) was created. But, the reason God needed to create a counterpart for Adam, was because animals were not counterparts. Meaning, God never created a beast with the ability to relate to man on his level.

(ADVICE)

Key Problem: If you are struggling with bestiality, this is an issue with abuse, security, low self-esteem and isolation. Sometimes, sex with animals is an escape from the pain and rejection that has come from people and/or experiences. Many withdraw into a life of isolation, and are drawn to childhood securities such as stuffed animals, and have an unhealthy security and affection towards animal figures or animals themselves. Animals become security blankets, replacing the security that only Jesus Christ can give, and this can so easily occur when one has been a victim of repeated abuse.

To overcome bestiality, pray, and ask God to help you apply the following steps:

(1) Repent- Turn away from this sin, and ask God to forgive you. (*Acts 3:19*)

(2) Counsel- Seek professional Christian counsel. (*Proverbs 11:14*)

(3) Church- Join a Bible teaching/living church. Let God nourish you through spiritual parents (Pastors) who will "speak" and "deposit" positive things into your life. (*Ephesians 4:11,12*)

(4) Ministry Groups- Join a men's/women's ministry. Allow God to develop the ability to have healthy relationships with people. (*Hebrews 10:25*)

(5) Word Study- Take a Bible and the *Strong's Concordance* and look up as many as many references as you can on animals and love (God's.)

For additional help and information See *Addiction, Fornication*

Bigamy

Bigamy- the act of being married to more than one person at the same time. In (*Genesis 2:24*), the scripture says, "*therefore a man shall leave his father and mother and be joined to his wife.*" Notice the emphasis on the singular use for man, not men being joined to a wife. Likewise, notice the singular use for wife, not wives being joined to a husband. In (*Matthew 19:4,5*) the scripture says, that God "*made them male and female*", we see another reference to the singular use of the marital terms. God intended to join one man, to one woman in a marriage. In some countries, bigamy is legal, but not in the United States. However, that statement was made to accent a vital point. Even, in places where the law has permitted this act, the Bible is clear, in (*Acts 5:29*), that "*we must obey God rather men.*" Allow me to give you some sound advice. In (*Genesis 29:30*), the scripture says, Jacob loved his two wives. But, "*he loved Rachel more than Leah.*" (*Matthew 19:5*), says, *"and the two shall become one flesh."* God never intended a marital relationship to exist outside of two people. A third party added to the relationship, creates problems. God created a man with the capacity, to handle only one woman, and a woman one man. This is why the Bible says, and the two, not the three, or the five, or the ten. You get the point. Bigamy, will always lead to somebody being loved less, or somebody being treated better. Because it is simply not, the arrangement of God.

(ADVICE)

Key Problem: If you are facing bigamy, this is an issue with loyalty and nurture. Generally, those who are struggling with this problem have not learned how to be committed, because they have had very little to no exposure to committed relationships. To overcome bigamy, pray, and ask God to help you apply the following steps: See *Key Problem*, under Adultery.

Clergy Immorality

Clergy Immorality- the act of sexual immorality among ministers. This is one of the most difficult and yet misunderstood subjects of sexual immorality that I've attempted to discuss. In (*2 Samuel 11*), the scriptures record the story of King David and his adulterous affair with Bethsheba.

However, the point that I would like to highlight of this infamous affair is David's misuse of power. David used his royal authority to have Bethsheba (who was married to Uriah) secretly brought to his house, where he committed adultery. Because David was the King, a man of power and authority, who would question the King? Who would challenge the King? No one. Not even Bethsheba who was suddenly taken from her house as if she was a prize claimed and collected for personal use. Sexual immorality among ministers/ leaders is about the abuse of power. It is the use of ministerial authority for personal gain or failure to use the same authority to promote the kingdom of God. A minister has been entrusted with the *"authority"* of God (*Hebrews 13:7,17, 1 Thessalonians 5:12,13.*) Failure to maintain proper focus of this delegated responsibility results in ministerial vulnerability.

In the book *"When a Leader Falls"* by Jan Winebrenner and Debra Fraizer, it is said that *"one out of eight pastors have admitted to having an affair."* Joe E. Trull, co-author of the book, *"Ministerial Ethics"* (1993) states, from his study of literature on clergy sexual abuse, that *"from 30 to 35 percent of ministers of all denominations admit to having sexual relationships-from inappropriate touching and kissing to sexual intercourse-outside of marriage."* Mr. Trull estimates that *"at least half of that contact occurs in pastoral counseling."* According to [*World Magazine*].

Today, 20 states have made sexual or therapeutic deception by professional counselors a crime. Typically, clergy are included in these statues if they are offering advice for emotional or mental problems." These are alarming, but hardcore facts. Behavioral specialist refer to this spiritual dilemma as therapeutic deception. The use of mental, emotional, or spiritual services for sexual gain.

In (*1 Samuel 2*), the Bible records the story of Eli, and his sons (a family of Israelite priests) who abused their positional power. The chapter states, the inappropriate behavior of Eli's priestly sons, who were having sex with women at the entrance of the Tabernacle (*sex at the Church; v22)* and stole the sacred offerings of God for selfish use (*vv12-17.*)

Sexual immorality is not new; ministers have been abusing power for centuries upon centuries. Ministers must be aware, that when God raises up a vessel, Satan devises a plan of destruction to make sure that the person never reaches the destiny of God. One of the most dangerous weapons that Satan has ever designed against mankind is sexual perversion. Even, in the beginning of man's origin, God created Adam first making him the person in authority, (*1 Timothy 2:11-13*) and Satan used sex appeal by tempting Adam through his wife (Eve) to disobey God.

Sexual temptation has no respect, not even for leadership. In fact, (*Proverbs 7:26*) teaches that sexual sin can destroy the strong. Moreover, a major contributor to immorality within church leadership is the seductive nature of sexual sin. This brings us to two significant figures of the Bible, who I call the "sex-twins." These two people are none other than Delilah and Jezebel. These women were known for their seductive natures, and the power they had over leadership (Judges *16, Revelation 2:20,21, 1 Kings 18:17-19.*)

However, they also represent two different characteristics of seduction. Delilah enticed with reservation causing Sampson to come after her. But, Jezebel enticed with aggression taking the initiative to go after the prophets of God. The spirit of these "twins" are prevalent against the clergy. Satan knows what turn you on. Some are turned on by being in charge; others are turned on by being pursued.

Regardless of your preference, the results are the same. Years of hard work, traded for a few minutes of cheap pleasure.

In the year 2002, the Catholic church was exposed with multiple sex scandals. Many fingered the Catholic church as if sexual scandals were a Catholic problem. The exposed immorality in the Catholic church was indicative of the blight in the entire church (Christendom), even the world. Sexual corruption is a people problem.

Nevertheless, if ministers have been endowed with the authoritative power of God, how can the clergymen get so weak? If ministers possess divine influence to do much good, how can they fall into so much bad?

The answer has been overlooked for ages. Ministers are human. We easily forget that beneath the clergy collar is a human being. The minister bleeds like everyone else, eats like everyone else, gets tired like everyone else, cries like everyone else, hurts like everyone else, and gets weak like anyone else. Moreover, many ministers are struggling with sexual immorality due to the lack of mentorship, or no mentorship at all.

Mentors are guides. Leaders need other leaders who will guide them in sexual integrity. Ministers need to live under the spiritual guidance of Senior-Ministers, who are living above sexual perversion, and will teach, correct and hold such leaders accountable. Apostle Paul exercised this principle of sexual mentorship with Pastor Timothy. (2 *Timothy 2:22.*) Yes, the minister is divine in mission, but, human in nature. And any human being is subject to failure. Sin is never excusable. But, I think we put too much faith in a man. At best we are imperfect. However, it is not my intention to make excuses for clerical immorality, but to present the facts with balance. If we are going to eliminate or reduce this problem, we must understand it, completely.

Sexual immorality in the clergy results in serious judgment. In (*1 Samuel 2:27-35,*) God judged Eli's priestly sons by defrocking (removing) them from the ministry, followed by death. God also judged Eli, because of his passive position towards his son's sins. Eli was also removed from the ministry, followed by death.

I want to list some common judgments of sexually immorality:

(a) Lost of ministry/employment-This act can result in excommunication from clergy privileges, and being fired from a job. (*1 Samuel 2*)

(b) Broken fellowship with God- This act can destroy your walk with God. This can send the ministry into a tailspin of mood swings, ranging from emptiness to confusion, failure, anger to hopelessness. (*Psalm 51*)

(c) Lost of integrity- This act can ruin your reputation, and even get your name placed on the sex offenders list. (*Proverbs 6:33*)

(d) Lost/Destruction of family- This act can eliminate your family or make it non-functional. (*2 Samuel 12*)

(e) Lawsuit- This act can result in being sued. The law calls ministers, clergy-counselors and relates to this behavior as "therapeutic deception."

(f) Jail-time- Many states have passed laws against this behavior. And ministers are going to jail at an alarming rate.

Considering the destructive power of sexual sin, how do we deal with it? I would like to present some vital steps that will aid in making a major difference. But, before I go into the steps, let me emphatically say that your mindset towards this situation is extremely critical. This mindset is two-fold. First, you must judge sexual sin. In (*Corinthians 5:7,9-13,*) the Apostle Paul is telling the church at Corinth to judge the sexual sin in the Church. The Greek word for judge is "krino" pronounced (kree-no), it means to sentence or punish. The Holy Spirit was saying to provide a constructive plan of punishment for the persons, who are caught in sexual sin. Second, remember, although we are to judge sexual sin, this is not the focus of God. God's goal is restoration, not condemnation. It is the intent of God to restore your life, and put you back together again. In (*Galatians 6:1,*) the Greek word for restore is "katartizo" pronounced (kat-ar-tid-zo), it means to complete thoroughly, to repair, to mend. It presents the illustration of a broken bone that has been restored, repaired or completely mended; where the bone works as if it was never broken. If you have fallen into sexual sin, God wants to judge you that he might fix you thoroughly and completely. Amen. Hence, our mindset towards sexual sin must be to judge with the intent to restore. (*St. John 8:3-11*)

The following steps are critical in correcting sexual sin in a congregational setting:

(a) Confrontation- Sexual sin is a deep seated problem and cannot be avoided, but must be swiftly approached. (*2 Samuel 12*)

(b) Repentance- There must be a turning away or separation from this sin, before God can begin deliverance. (*Psalm 51, 2 Samuel 12.*) Demand that any and all involvement is broken off, immediately.

(c) Sitting- A fallen minister loses the rights to ministerial privileges until sufficient restoration has occurred. The ministry of a minister is based on character and integrity (*1 Timothy 3.*) This is what people follow and admire: the God in you, not the you in you. Once you lose that, you lose people. Sin destroys character (Romans 6:23, Genesis 3.) Thus a minister needs time to rebuild and demonstrate loss character. The time to re-appoint a minister back to office, is based on individual progress and the Ministerial Covering (Authorities) that the minister is under. Many ministerial boards have designated a minimum 6 months to 1 year as a restoration period. However, each authority group must pray and be led by God.

(d) Accountability- The fallen minister should have a group of authorities (Restoration Committee) that he or she must answer to. There should be regular reporting and monitoring of the minister's progress. Leaders need leaders. Remember, power has been abused. Submitting to power helps challenge and correct the distorted view of authority. (*Hebrews 13:7,17 Acts 15:1,2*)

(e) Counsel- The fallen minister should be counseled by experienced leadership. (*Proverbs 11:14*)

(f) Restitution- The fallen minister is in debt to the people he or she injured Sin is never private. Your decisions affects your entire world. People treat you the way they see you. If they hear something bad about you, it will change the way they see and treat you. This is particularly true for a Christian. A Christian is a connected part in the body of Christ. (*1Corinthians 12:12-27*) and what you do affects other Christians. Restitution means paying back the thing taken. Sexual sin causes a lot of lost. A fallen minister must put back the trust, respect, unity, peace, and everything that was destroyed (*Exodus 22:1-3.*) This helps the injured heart to heal.

(g) Time- It is important that a fallen minister does not return to the ministry before restoration has been completed. It will be devastating for both the minister and the congregation. The key to determining readiness is character or the heart. Jesus said "*a tree is known by it's fruit*" (*Matthew 7:20.*) Fruit does not come up over night; it needs time. True fruit is only revealed over a period of consistent godly behavior. (*St. John 14:23*)

It is important to note, that a minister's restoration should occur within his local church. The minister's own church should help aid in the recovery process. Some people may disagree, and prefer to send the minister away to a special center, or program.

This brings us to another critical area of this discussion; forgiveness. The minister has the responsibility to change, but the church has the responsibility to forgive. After you have been shattered by a leader you trusted, admired and looked up to; how do you forgive? You feel angry, failed, tricked, lied to, confused, blame, unforgiveness, and insecurity. How?

49

In (*Luke 17:3-5,*) Jesus taught a powerful lesson on forgiveness. Forgiveness means to pardon or release. After Jesus taught this lesson, in verse 3, the disciples asked the Lord to increase their faith. After Jesus taught on the awesome responsibility of forgiving someone, who has hurt you, the disciples said Lord we need faith, or Lord, help us "*trust in you to accomplish this*. You will have to trust God to get past this type of pain. How? Allow me to give you some steps that are relevant to forgiving ministers:

(A) Forgiveness is the will of God- Forgiveness is not a suggestion or human opinion; it is the will of God. It is not conditional. God says forgive, period. This means if a person never apologizes, or makes things right, I am obligated to forgive or release them. Why? It's the will of God. (*Mark 11:25*)

(B) God forgave you- In the cross or death of Jesus Christ, God provided the grounds to forgive you of your sins. This also released the law of sowing and reaping "*whatever a person sows they will also reap.*" Because God gave forgiveness to us, He has a right to ask us to forgive. (*Ephesians 4:32*)

(C) Uncover sin- Exposure of sin must be done discreetly. In a setting where a congregation is aware through rumors that something has happened to one of the leaders; the people deserves a tactful explanation. Having an understanding that a leader has fallen equips the congregation to better handle the problem and begin to move forward with healing. People cannot heal left in darkness and confusion. (*1 Corinthians 5, James 5:16*)

(D) Express grief- People must be given the opportunity to express their frustration, anger, questions, etc. The leaders should call a Church meeting. (*Ecclesiastes 3:4*)

(E) Multiple Leadership Accountability- The congregation needs to know that the problem is being dealt with through more than one person of integrity and authority (Board, Ministerial Staff, Mediator.) (*Acts 15:6 James 5:16*)

(F) Counseling- The congregation must be given the opportunity to receive experienced counsel. (*Proverbs 11*)

(G) New Leadership- The congregation must see a change in leadership before healing will occur. This means a restored leader or replacement leader. (*2 Samuel 12, 1 Corinthians 5:6,7*)

These steps will greatly aid the victims of clergy immorality in receiving the forgiving power and restoration of the Lord.

(ADVICE)

Key Problem: If you are struggling with clergy immorality as a minister, this is an issue with abuse of authority and mentoring. It is power used selfishly for your own gain or power that you failed to use for the Kingdom of God. Most of the leaders struggling with sexual sin, do not have role models who constantly impart integrity and accountability into their lives. Remember, that your decision is not private. It will impact others. If you are married, you have damaged your spouse, and if you have children, they have also been damaged. Counseling and healing is necessary.

For more direction on how to overcome clergy immorality as a individual/congregation, pray, and ask God to help you apply the following steps:

(A) Start a Sexual Education Ministry

(B) Establish a Sexual Abuse Reporting Policy (See Below)

(C) Publish written guidelines for the congregation (This puts sexual prowlers on alert, and raises the sexual awareness of the church)

Consider the following guidelines:

1. It must be reported to ministerial authorities. (*Acts 15:6,29*)

2. There must be witnesses or solid evidence. (*1 Timothy 5:19*)

3. It must be reported with a sincere attitude. (*Galatians 6:1*)

4. It should be kept confidential (written and sealed) followed by a meeting. (*1Corinthians 14:40*)

5. There should be a reasonable established a period of time to resolve the matter. And a set time to report back to the reporting person on the status of the situation. (*Ephesians 5:16*)

(D) Conduct a thorough background check of ministerial candidates.

(E) Implement a probation period for ministerial candidates.

(F) Select clergy with training in sexual education.

Compromise

Compromise- the act of putting one's self at danger or risk. In (*Matthew 4:7*), the scripture says, that "*you should not tempt the Lord your God.*" The word "*tempt*" comes from the Greek word "ekpiradzo" pronounced (*ek-pi-rad-zo.*) In this particular scripture, the word means to try the patience of God, to take advantage of God's goodness, by needlessly placing one's self in danger. It simply means placing yourself in a situation, that you know could get you in trouble, but expecting God to cover you. That's called tempting God, or compromise.

Many people have gotten themselves into sexual traps because of compromise. My wife, and I have counseled countless numbers of people, who have expressed, not understanding how they stumbled into circumstances of sexual temptation, which changed their whole life. One of the most common traps, are church leaders who minister to people of the opposite sex, without ground rules. In (*James 5:17,*) the scripture says, "*Elijah was a man subject to like passions as we are.*" Elijah was a prophet (*spiritual leader*) and he had like passions or the same nature as every human being.

Often times people, including the leaders themselves, do not understand that leaders are very human. We do have power, but we also have limitations. We eat, sleep, hurt, and bleed like anyone else. We can't walk around with the superman complex, that "it can't happen to me." In (*Judges 16:19,*) the scriptures teach that Sampson, an Israelite judge (*spiritual leader*) known for his great strength, and might, was asleep on Delilah's lap. Delilah was a philistine, and seductress. The Philistines were an ungodly nation, and enemies to God's people (the Israelites.) The scripture says, in verse 4, of this 16th chapter, that Sampson loved Delilah. But the Bible never says, that she loved him. Sampson pursued a woman, who did not love God. Placing his entire life in jeopardy. Unfortunately, the end result of this compromising decision was the lost of his life, and ministry. Leaders don't risk your investment (ministry.)

You have come to far, and God has given you to much, to risk years of hard work, over minutes of sexual pleasure. Another common trap, is a married spouse, who is unhappy at home. But, enjoys talking over lunch about her marital problems, with a co-worker of the opposite sex. In (*Proverbs 7:6-27,*) the scripture teaches, that their was a man who was drawn into sexual temptation, because he was both curious, and lacking in understanding (*verse 7.*)

In many relational downfalls, people will put themselves at risk, simply because they are curious of what it would be like, with some new thing. There are certain things in life, you don't need to know. You don't need to know the places, the people, or the opportunities that can give you all the sexual fun, you can handle. Its been said that "curiosity killed the cat." What you don't know could save you. Spouses who compromise their marriage, are usually searching for something that is not at home, and show a lack of good judgment, or understanding. In whatever situation, you find yourself. "*Give no place* (opportunity) *to the Devil*".

(ADVICE)

Key Problem: If you are struggling with compromise, this is an issue with risk. Some are willing to lower their standards to risk valuable things. To overcome compromise, pray and ask God to help you apply the following steps:

1. Repent- Turn away from this sin, and ask God to forgive you. (*Acts 3:19*)

2. Avoid gambling in every form of the word. (*Proverbs 16:33*)

3. Avoid sexual fantasies. (*2 Corinthians 10:5*)

4. Develop a sensitive heart for godliness- the closer to God a person becomes, the harder it is to risk the goodness of God. (*Acts 13:22, James 4:8*)

Cross-Dressing

Cross-dressing- the act of a person dressing in the clothes of the opposite sex to create sexual arousal. In (*Deuteronomy 22:5,*) the scripture says, "*a woman should not wear anything that pertains to a man, nor shall a man put on a woman's garment.*" This scripture was giving by God, to help protect sexual balance. God intended each sex, to maintain their original identity. Clothes present an image, and images send messages.

In (*Genesis 38:14-16,*) the scriptures teach that one day Judah saw his daughter-in-law (*Tamar*) in a public place. And did not recognize her, due to the way she was dressed. In verse 14, the Bible teaches that Tamar's husband had just died. And in that day widows dressed a certain way. Tamar, purposing to go unnoticed changed her clothes, and covered her face with a veil or light piece of clothing (the manner in which temple prostitutes dressed, in that day.) When her father-in-law (*Judah*) saw her, he unknowingly approached her to buy sex, thinking that he had advanced a prostitute. Unaware, that this was his own daughter-in-law. What happened? Her "clothes" presented an image, and sent a message. Images and messages are not wrong.

When you put on your clothes, you have to stop and ask yourself what am I saying to the world?

Concerning clothing, I believe that are two main things to consider. First, does my choice of dressing bring confusion? In (*1Corinthians 14:33,*) the scripture says "*God is not the author of confusion.*" When a man dresses like a woman (*transvestite*), that is very confusing. It is a man inside of clothes that were designed to present the body and face of a woman. This reveals confusion and it confuses people.

Most of this confusion starts in childhood. Where, perhaps a little boy spent too much time playing with female toys. Like dolls, for example. Or Perhaps, a child is involved in role-playing. Where a little boy dresses in a dress, panties, stockings and high heels, to play the role of a housewife. Or a little girl, who borrows her little brother's suit to dress like a man, to play the role of a husband.

Imagine these children having no adult supervision, playing this type of commonly played game, everyday as an after school pass-time. It is very likely that seeds of confusion will get planted in their understanding of sexuality. Remember, (*Galatians 6:7*) says " *whatsoever a man sow , he will also reap.*" A lot of our adult behavior, started in our child behavior. Hence, we must watch behavior that could confuse who we are.

Secondly, when I put on my clothes what type of image am I presenting to the world? the scripture says, in (*Matthew 5:16*) *"Let your light so shine before men, that they may see your good works and glorify your Father in heaven."* Our *"good works"* or lifestyle is our light. When a man dresses like a woman or a woman dresses like a man, that is not a good image being presented. People should be able to look at our works, including the way we dress and see God (*1 Timothy 2:9.*) Apostle Paul summed it up like this *"put on the Lord Jesus Christ."*

(ADVICE)

Key Problem: If you are struggling with cross-dressing; this is an issue gender identity. It is discovering who you are, and obeying God. To overcome cross-dressing; pray, and ask God to help you apply the following steps: See Key Problem, under Homosexuality.

Dating (Ungodly)

Dating (*non-biblical*)- courtship, or the act of attracting, or gaining favor for the purpose of a relationship. Dating is not a sin. I believe that dating helps prepare one for their soul-mate. However, my focus is on the type of dating that is contrary to the word of God, resulting in lots of sexual problems, and immorality. In this context, there are basically two types of dating: a Christian dating a non-Christian, and a Christian or non-Christian who dates according to their own rules.

First, a Christian who dates a person who is not a Christian, is breaking some serious ground rules. In (*2 Corinthians 6:14-18,*) the scriptures teach **"be not unequally yoked."** The Greek word for unequally yoked is "heterozugeo" pronounced *(het-er-od-zoog-eh-o)* which means to be different or contrast.

I know people are different in personalities. But, when two people are looking at sharing a life of intimacy, there should not be a difference in the nature, lifestyles or foundations of the two people. This passage of scripture bears confirmation to this truth. Notice, verse 14 further says, *"what fellowship has righteousness with unrighteousness? And what communion has light with darkness"*?

The point that God is making is that a Christian and a non-Christian has two lives that are so different, that it is impossible to unite. There will be an unequal-ness, an unbalance or contrast.

I have counseled countless numbers of people who have dared to take this challenge. And yes, they too added themselves to the untold numbers of people, who attempted to build a life with two different value systems (God versus self), only to be crushed under the weight of their own sins.

In (*Deuteronomy 7:1-4*) the scriptures teach that the Israelites were to avoid entering into marriage with pagan nations. In verse 4, we are told the unavoidable danger of Israel, *"turning away"* from God, due to relationships with a non-spiritual people. In (*1 Kings 11:1-3,*) the scriptures teach that in verse 1, *"Solomon loved many "strange" or "foreign (ungodly) women"*, and the result of these unequal relationships, verse 4 says *"his wives [turned] away his heart after other gods."* King Solomon, was turned away from God. This is the ultimate reason, for Christians to avoid dating non-Christians.

The second type of dating, is when Christians or non-Christians used dating practices contrary to the word of God. One of the most common mistakes made by a lot of people, is to date with no intention of seeking marriage. Many people have asked the question, why doesn't the Bible say much about dating. The simple explanation, is that God is ultimately interested in people spending "life" together, not "time" together. When you meet someone of interest, God doesn't want you seeking a boyfriend or girlfriend, but rather a husband or wife.

Nevertheless, there are other common mistakes that people make while dating. To begin, people put too much emphasis on the "body." Don't get me wrong, it's nothing wrong with being physically attracted to someone. The body is the first line of impression. But, unfortunately many people stop at this line, and never get to the personality of an individual. In (*2 Corinthians 4:16,*) the scripture says "*our outward man is perishing.*" The Apostle Paul calls the outward man the body. The body is perishing or wasting away. This means that over a period of time, a person's body can go through some serious changes. Which means, that good looks are subject to change into bad looks. Therefore, one should take the advice of Apostle Peter, who taught in (*1 Peter 3:3,4,*) that the human spirit does not fade away and when the spirit of a man, has godly traits, that human spirit is precious or priceless in the sight of God. This means that real beauty, is on the inside of a person, not on the outside.

However, I want to broaden the concept of beauty, by speaking in reference to a person's life as a whole. We spoke of the focus of beauty, being inward, but I want to speak about beauty as a whole to answer one of the most common questions in the arena of relationships; how do I attract a potential soul mate? In a nutshell, you have to become beautiful. Beauty is power. People are drawn to beautiful things. Whether you are a man or a woman, I want you to understand that nobody refuses a beautiful person.

To define the nature of beauty, allow me to start with an illustration. For example, if you were looking to buy a home, you would not be looking for one thing about the house. But, you would look for the type of home (brick or wood), how many bedrooms? how many bathrooms? is there a basement? size of the yard, what is the neighborhood like? how close are the schools? how many shopping stores in the area? are there any parks? and etc. What would make the house attractive is the multiple features. Real beauty is also having several features about your life. Being able to bring a lot to the table. The following is some general advice on becoming a beautiful person:

(1) Personality- Become sweet. (sensitive, thoughtful, fun, flexible.) This will add flavor to you life. (*Esther 2:12-18.*)

(2) Appearance- Stay well groomed. Keep good hygiene. Maintain physical fitness (it is the first thing people see.) (*Romans 12:1, Song of Solomon 4, 5:10-16.*)

(3) Possessions- Accumulate assets (house, car, job, phone, investments.) It adds worth to your life. (*Genesis 13:1,2.*)

(4) Knowledge- Be intelligent. Gain a basic grasp on life. (1 Peter *3:7.*)

(5) Skills- Be resourceful. Have the ability to help. (cook, fix a car, make light repairs on a house, manage money, run a business, give good ADVICE.) (*Exodus 36:1, Genesis 13:1,2.*)

(6) Goals- Have an aim. Go after something that will benefit your life. (Proverbs *6:6-10.*)

(7) Stability- Learn to set a goal, and stay with it. (a decision, job, business, bills.) (*James 1:7,8.*)

(8) Communicator- Learn to be a good conversationalist. People like to talk. Communication is one of the greatest ingredients that feed strong relationships. Words are vehicles that transport needs, and an understanding of people. (*Song of Solomon 4, 5:10-16.*)

(9) Reputation- Keep a clean life. Stay virtuous. No one wants to touch things that have been corrupted. (*2 Samuel 13:12,13.*)

10) God- Keep Jesus Christ at the center of your life. Ask God for direction, and have faith. (faith is action, act on the biblical ADVICE.) God is the real match-maker. (*Genesis 2:22, Matthew 7:7, James 2:20.*)

These are things that create "beauty", and will unquestionably make "anybody" a number 10. However, another common mistake during dating, is excessive touching or petting. Petting is the act of kissing and caressing (intimate touching.) Touching is very powerful, and it can be used in either a positive or negative way. God has designed the body with millions of nerve-endings. Subsequently, when the body is touched in certain places (hands, face, lips, back , legs , genitals, etc.), a relay of power goes off . That little touch, triggers a nerve, which sends a signal to the brain, which causes a signal to be released by the brain to your sex-drive and the rest is history.

I would like to also, suggest to be careful about dating by yourself, verses a group setting. Most people are not ready for it. Remember, you are human, and the human nature likes comfort. This is why most people prefer to be in a close space, a quiet room, or some where private, because it is very comfortable and satisfying to the human nature. The Bible says in (*Ephesians 4:27*) "*give no place to the Devil.*" The word place means opportunity. In other words, anything that might give Satan an opportunity or control over my life should be avoided.

Another common mistake, is fornication yes fornication. Sex before marriage. Many people fall for the old "If you love me, why wait?" trick. Did you know the Bible teaches, in (*Hebrews 13:4*), that God will judge the fornicator (whoremonger) and adulterer. This explains why people who have sex before marriage, can't seem to get the relationship off the ground. There is no joy, lots of arguing and a bunch of confusion. What you have is a case of divine judgment. The relationship has been judged and will never work, until things are made right. No Fornication.

True love, or interest will wait. In (*Genesis 29:20-30*) the scriptures teach, that Jacob loved Rachel, and because he loved her, he was willing to wait 14 years to have her in marriage, and romance. Waiting is a true sign of love. What you have to offer is valuable. Don't sell your self short. Wait.

(ADVICE)

Key Problem: If you are struggling with ungodly dating, this is an issue of self-value and compromise. It is the act of selling yourself short. God is beautiful, and desires to replace your unattractiveness (low-self esteem) with the "beauty of the Lord." (*Psalms 90:17*)

To overcome ungodly dating, pray, and ask God to help you apply the following steps:

1. Repent- Turn away from this sin, and ask God to forgive you. (*Acts 3:19.*)

2. Focus on becoming a strong single. (*1Corinthians 7:32, Matthew 25:23.*)

3. Don't date until you are ready for marriage. (*1Corinthians 7:1,9.*)

4. Understand God's requirements for marriage. (*1Peter 3:7.*)

5. Look for a demonstration of marital qualities. (*Matthew 7:20.*)

6. Allow lots of time in observing the heart of a potential spouse. (*Genesis 29:20-30.*)

Erotic Dancing

Erotic Dancing- The act of dancing to create sexual arousal. In

(*Matthew 14:6,*) the scripture says "*but when Herod's birthday was kept, the daughter of Herodias danced before them and pleased Herod.*" In the text the word "*danced*" means a rowing or circular motion, and here it here it meant a seductive or erotic dance. Thus, the daughter of Herodias performed a sexual dance for the King. Erotic dancing is about the art of temptation. The strength of this type of dancing lies in the dancer's ability to tempt or arouse the client. This is why many dancers are referred to as teases. Whether it is a show at the club, bar, house party, lap dancing, stripping or doing the skin tight (dancing in skin tight clothing) it is against the word of God to both tempt or be tempted.

In studying the life of erotic dancers; when a dancer is asked, what makes you dance?, most of them say money. It is an economical greed that drives the dancer to do what they do. In (1 Timothy *6:10,*) the scripture says "*for the love [greed] of money is the root of all kinds of evil.*" A greed for money will drive a person to do some dishonorable things. Dancers get paid very well, but most of them will tell you if it was not for the money they would not do it. In fact, most dancers are ashamed of their job, but will tell you "it pays the bills."

I believe another general reason for erotic dancing is attention. Many dancers are seduced by their own seduction. There is a thrill that a dancer gets to see the excitement that is produced in the customer(s.) In that moment the dancer feels the power of controlling someone else's behavior. It is an ego trip that leads to a cheap thrill. Dancers put themselves in positions to be stumbling blocks. In (*Romans 14:13,*) the scripture says "*not to put a stumbling block in our brother's way.*" A stumbling block is something that causes a person to trip or fall into sin. Dancers promote temptation. However, you can't talk about dancing, without eventually talking about music. If the dancing don't get you eventually the music will.

Music is an extremely powerful source of seduction. One of the reasons why, is because (*Ezekiel 28:13*) teaches that Satan is musical in his very nature. This is why some of the most skillful and talented music is also seductive, because Satan is the mastermind behind the scenes. Whether you are driving in your car, resting at home, or laboring at work, be careful about listening to sensuous music, it will seduce you. Just imagine some sexy music behind a sexy dancer, it is a powerful combination. And it is these electrifying dynamics that are at work in the atmosphere of erotic dancing.

In the book of (*Exodus 32:17-21,*) we have the same scenario, dirty dancing. Joshua heard a different sound in the camp. Erotic music carries it's own sound. It was not the spiritual sound that Israel was accustomed to, but rather the sound of seduction. And when Joshua approached the camp the people were singing, dancing, and caught up in sexual seduction. Moreover, it is interesting to note that before Israel discovered the invention of musical instruments, their voices were used musically (*Exodus 15:1.*)

Thus, this strange sound in the camp of Israel was music that was created by their voices along with dancing that did not glorify God. Nevertheless, this industry aids the perverted view of sexuality. Men and women become mere objects for sexual pleasure. It encourages unfaithfulness. After a couple of drinks and a couple of dances, many are tempted to release the build up of sexual energy by cheating with the most available person. Ultimately, erotic dancing destroys a family, and many homes are ruined because of these establishments. Furthermore, erotic dancing does not build a good or respectable work history. Most employers outside of the industry do not respect these type of working skills. If you decided to change jobs, due to physical challenges, dissatisfaction or a plain old desire for a change of pace, It would be difficult to do off of this type of work history.

(ADVICE)

Key Problem: If you are struggling with erotic dancing; this is an issue with low self-esteem and seduction. Let God help you understand the purpose of the body. (*Romans 12:1*) says, "*present your bodies a living sacrifice, holy, acceptable to God*" Your body was created for the pleasure of God. (*1 Corinthians 6:19*) says, "*or do you not know that your body is the temple of the Holy Spirit who is in you.*" God desires to make your body a temple or a property of worship. Let God have your body and your heart. You do not deserve to be an object for Satan, but a dwelling for God.

To overcome erotic dancing, pray, and ask God to help you apply the following steps:

1. Repent- Turn away from this sin, and ask God to forgive you. (*Acts 3:19.*)

2. Word Study -Take a Bible and a Strong's Concordance and look up as many references as you can on music and body. (*2 Timothy 2:15.*)

3. Read (*Psalm 150*) to understand God's ultimate purpose for music.

4. Avoid sensuous music. (*Hebrews 12:1,2, Matthew 14:6.*)

5. Avoid clubbing/partying. (*Psalm 1:1, Galatians 5:21*)

6. Avoid seductive people. (*1 Corinthians 15:33.*)

7. Church- Join a Bible teaching/living church. Allow God to nourish you through spiritual parents (Pastors) who will speak and deposit positive things into your life. (*Hebrews 10:25.*)

Fatal Attraction

Fatal Attraction- a sexual interest that results in, or is associated with the taking of a life. In (*2 Samuel 11:1-17,*) the scriptures teach that King David had sexual interest in a married woman by the name of Bathsheba. David committed adultery with Bathsheba, which resulted in her becoming pregnant. David had the option of coming clean with his sin. But, desired Bathsheba so much, that he had her husband (Uriah) killed to cover up his sin. This was an attraction that led to a fatality (death.)

I would like to identify some of the most basic characteristics that can create fatal attraction. But, before I proceed I would like to point out the fact that fatal attraction can also, be expressed through sex-murders. This is the brutal act of being sexually aroused by the taking of a human life. This generally takes on the form of rape, followed by the murder of the same victim. Some murderers will wait until their victim is dead and perform sex acts on the victim known as necrophilia (sex with the dead.) Strikingly, these various expressions of fatal attraction come under the general umbrella of sexual attraction associated with death.

Nevertheless, lets take a look at six things that I believe are potential signs for a fatal attraction. The first sign is anger. Anger is that most commonly displayed, emotion of intense displeasure. In (*Proverbs 29:22,*) the writer Solomon, tells us that *"an angry man stirs up strife"*, this means, when anger is in control it creates conflicts and division, *"and a furious man increases in transgression"* anger will cause a person to commit a pile of wrong. Moreover, (*Proverbs 19:19*) says *"a man of great wrath (anger) shall suffer punishment: for if you deliver him, yet you must do it again."* Anger can cause negative repetitious behavior, leading one into a cycle of uncontrollable destruction.

The second sign is abuse. In (*Genesis 16:5,6*) the scripture says, Sarah (*Sarai*) dealt "*harshly*" with Hagar. The word harshly in the Hebrew language means abusive. Abusive behavior always express hard and insensitive actions towards people. Don't allow this sign to be mistaking for love.

The third sign is controlling. In the book of (*1 Kings chapters 18-21*) and particularly chapter 21:25, Jezebel the wife of King Ahab, is clearly seen as a controlling wife. Jezebel controlled her husband to the point of making most of his decisions. Does this sound familiar? King Ahab was not allowed to be his own self. Whether you are single or married, you are expected to always retain your singleness.

Did you know the word single means unique, different, one of a kind. In (*Genesis 1:27,*) the scripture says, "*God created him; male and female He created them.*" Notice the difference in the spelling of the words used to identify the first two human beings: male and female. We have two males. But one has "fe" or the ability to carry a fetus. This of course is the woman. However, God named these two people differently, because He created the man and woman to function uniquely and distinctly, different from one another. Therefore, you have a right to be an individual.

The fourth sign is jealousy. In (*Genesis 37:5-28,*) particularly verses 8 and 11, the scriptures teach that Joseph was "*hated*" by his brothers and was the object of their "*jealousy*." The result of his brothers' jealousy was very cruel treatment. Jealousy is generally associated with hatred, and will disregard even the closest of ties, and people who play very important roles. Keep in mind, that these were his own brothers.

The fifth sign is loss. In the book of (*Ruth 1:3-18*), Ruth loses her husband after ten years of marriage and develops a very close relationship with her mother-in-law (Naomi.) When Naomi talked about departing from her daughters-in-law that they might return to their home lands for a better chance of remarrying and living productive lives, Ruth clung to Naomi and wouldn't let her go. Ruth's loss of her husband made her sensitive to the potential loss of her mother-in-law (*Naomi.*) Loss can make a person sensitive to loss.

The sixth sign is unforgiveness. If a person has a history of pain, where they have always been the target of rejection, abuse, and humiliation; it can become difficult for them to forgive. A person who struggles with forgiving someone for wrong committed against them, is not ready for a relationship. Life is filled with too many flaws. (*Matthew 18.*)

(ADVICE)

Key Problem: If you are struggling with fatal Attraction; this is an issue with abuse and nurture. A person experiencing fatal attraction is a victim of past hurt. Generally, their is also a history of improper or inadequate parental care. To overcome fatal attraction, pray, and ask God to help you apply the following steps:

(Victim):

(a) Watch for early signs- Pay attention to signs of abuse. (Ephesians 5:15)

(b) Break off the relationship- An abusive relationship that will not change should not continue. (*2 Corinthians 6:17,18*)

(c) Intercede- Pray for the abuser. Pray for salvation/deliverance. (*Matthew 9:38*)

(d) Take precaution- Protect yourself. This may involve the police (*Romans 13:1-7*)

(e) Seek counsel- Get professional Christian counsel. (*Proverbs*

24:6)

(Abuser)

(a) Repent- Let go of the person you are victimizing. (*Acts 3:19*)

(b) Church- Join a Bible teaching/living church. Allow God to nourish your void through spiritual parents (Pastors.)

(c) Ministry Groups- Join a men's/women's ministry, and learn to build healthy relationships

(d) Counsel- Get professional Christian counsel. (*Proverbs 24:6*)

(e) Word Study- Take a Bible and a Strong's Concordance and look up as many references as you can on love (God's.)

Fornication

Fornication -This word is commonly misunderstood by most people. Fornication carries a two-fold meaning: first, it is the act of sex between two unmarried people.

Second, it has a general meaning of any ungodly sex. This is the truest meaning of the word (*1 Thessalonians 4:3.*) It comes from the Greek word porneia pronounced (por-nee-a.) Fornication is used in various ways throughout the scriptures.

Lets take a look at some of these multiple uses. In (*Matthew 19:4-6,*) fornication is called (adultery), (*1Corinthians 5:1-5*) (incest), (*Romans 1:26-28*) (homosexuality), (*St. John 8:37-41*) (the birth of illegitimate children.) Although, fornication is described by different words in the English language, the same Greek word "porneia" is used in each instance. Hence, this tells us that pornea or fornication has multiple uses. In the scriptures, fornication is presented as a dangerous word. The Bible says, in (*1Corinthians 6:18*), "*flee fornication.*" The word flee in this context means to run from danger. The Holy Spirit is clearly saying, that fornication from the onset may appear to be exciting, but is a very dangerous experience.

This is why the Bible says, in (*Hebrews 13:4*), *"fornicators and adulterers God will judge."* No other sin has released the wrath of God like sexual sin. In (*Genesis 19*), God destroyed two cities (Sodom and Gomorrah) due to sexual sin. In (*1Corinthians 10:8*), 23,000 people died due to fornication.

This would explain why the Apostle Paul says, that *"all other sins are without the body, but he that commits fornication sins against his own body"* (*1Corinthians 6:18*) In (*1 Corinthians 7:2*), the Corinthians were told, *"let a man not touch a woman."* The word touch in this context means to light a fire. Hence, the word of God is clear that fornication should be avoided at all cost. Because without the Spirit of God, it is a fire that cannot be put out. In fact, most of the time a person becomes sexually aroused, it is difficult to exercise control.

A person is overwhelmed by hormones. For, a hormone is a cell that has the ability to stir or create impulse. Your hormones literally create passionate impulses and stir up sexual behavior. This impulse or fire has the ability to easily spread. And one of the greatest ways that fornication spreads, is through people.

This is why the word of God cautions us against *"keeping company with fornicators"* (*1 Corinthians 5:9*) If you hang around people who talk a lot about sexual experiences, tell sexual jokes, dress provocative, present themselves in a flirtatious manner, is always looking for sexual opportunities, it is without question, you will become sexually perverted.

This is what happens to people who are living under a generational curse of sexual immorality. For example, In (*2 Samuel 11*), King

David committed adultery, his son Amnon raped his own sister (*2 Samuel 13*), his son Absalom committed adultery against his father, by having sex with David's concubines (*2 Samuel 16:20-23*), his son King Solomon became a sexual addicted (a thousand women for his own sexual pleasure) (*2 Kings 11.*)

This is a clear example of sexual immorality passing from one generation to another. In (*Hosea 1:2*), there is a similar reference, about prophet Hosea's wife (Gomer) who was a harlot or prostitute, who produced children that became harlots. Essentially this same generational principle led to a family of prostitutes.

Your environment determines your destiny. That's why it is important to watch your children; particularly, their peers. Our children are surrounded by a fornication-society. As sexual immorality pervades our teenage population, alarming signs have been the result: unwanted pregnancies, sexually transmitted diseases, school drop-outs, shacking up, premature marriages, job loss and it goes on. Without the intervention of God, the young people of today will pave a perverted path for the youth of tomorrow.

However this generational curse can be stopped by the generational blessing. If a company of fornicators can produce a company of fornicators, what will a company of virgins do? A people who have never polluted themselves with sexual immorality. Or a people (second-virginity virgins) who lost their virginity, but repented and sold out to God to live a sex-free life until marriage. A people of sexual standards will produce people of sexual standards, ultimately resulting in the elimination of this satanic norm that sex before marriage is normal. Remember, a generational curse is reversed by a generation of obedience. (Deuteronomy *28.*)

Ironically, the scriptures teach that virginity has not only been a mark of virtue, but also of value. Contrary to popular opinion which says that being a virgin is a square; a virgin is of great value.

In (*Exodus 22: 16, 17*) the Bible teaches that a virgin was worth money. A dowry was paid to the father prior to the marriage of a virgin. But, if a woman lost her virginity outside of marriage there was no dowry (bride-payment.)

This tells us that a virgin was held in honor and great value. Even to this day, when a person is discovered as having a reputation of sleeping with a lot of people, they are held in low esteem. Society practices fornication, and frowns upon it at the same time. What irony. Don't let the devil trick you out of your virginity. Whether you are a literal virgin or a person who decided to give up sexual immorality and live as a virgin (*second-virginity*), saying yes to temptation takes value from your life, but saying no adds value to your life.

Did you know, that a female virgin has what is known as a hymen which is a thin layer of mucous membrane that partially covers the opening of the vagina? The hymen is also like a seal. It is as if God is telling us that sex is sealed until the day of marriage. Moreover, when a virgin has sex for the first time the hymen is usually broken causing light bleeding from the vaginal area. This may sound a bit gross, but it's actually apart of God's natural design for the first act of sexual intercourse. Sex is suppose to occur for the first time inside of the marriage covenant, where the wife bleeds from her vagina on to the penis of her husband, reflecting two significant biblical principals: the blood covenant and the first fruits offering. In (*Leviticus 17:11*), the Bible says that life is in the blood.

The word covenant means to come together or to join. Thus, the breaking of the hymen is a blood joining, or a life joining. It is meant to say that my blood or my life is joined to your life forever.

The "*first fruits offering*" has always reflected that God is first or superior. (*Proverbs 3:9,10, Matthew 6:33.*) The breaking of the hymen inside the marriage says, that God is Lord over your love life. And this is what causes God to bless the romance of the relationship.

In light of understanding the significance of the blood covenant and the first fruits offering, imagine the confusion that is created, when a person has sex with someone that they're not married to, or someone that they don't even know. You could "bond" with the wrong person. (that's another story see Soul-ties.)

Nevertheless, fornication is not restricted to a population, race or belief. It is a global problem. Even in the church world, the ecclesia, the "*called out.*" This problem of sexual immorality is calling in, the people of God to a realm of unlimited perversion. Throughout the word of God, sexual sin has been a challenge even for the saints of God.

In the Old Testament some significant references are (*Leviticus 18, Judges 14,16, 2 Samuel 11, 1 Kings 11:1-3, Hosea 1;*) most of the books in the New Testament deal with sexual sin, and almost half of the New Testament deals with the Church facing sexual sin issues (*Matthew 5:28, St. John 8:3, Acts 15:29, Romans 1:26,27, 1Corinthians 5:1, Galatians 5:19, Ephesians 5;5, Phillipppians 3:19, Colossians 3:5, 1 Thessalonians 4:3, 2 Timothy 2:22, Hebrews 13:4, 2 Peter 2:14, Revelation 2:21,22.*)

The purpose of showing the involvement of the Church with sexual sin is to show the seriousness of fornication. If the people of God, who are equipped with the power of God can be deceived and weakened into a place of compromise, this should awaken us to the fact that sexual sin must be taken serious.

In a nutshell, here is what fornication does to a person's life; (*Proverbs 6:32,33*), teaches that fornication causes "wounds."

This word means a blow. Every time a person's commits fornication, it delivers a crushing blow to their life. This is why what many think is a one night stand, ends up being a life time scar. This also explains why most people can't seem to resist sexual sin. Once fornication delivers it's blow, you are now crushed, fragmented, and weakened. Fornication weakens you every time you commit it. The following are some of the most common blows of sexual sin:

(1)   Broken fellowship with God. (*Psalm 51:10-12.*)

(2)   Destroys the soul. (*Proverbs 6:32.*)

(3)   Cheapens sex. (1 Kings *11:1-3.*)

(4)   Subject to sexually transmitted diseases. (*Proverbs 5:11, Revelation 2:21,22.*)

(5)   Pregnancy. (*2 Samuel 11.*)

(6)   Soul-ties. (*1Corinthians 6:16,17.*)

(7)   Transfer of evil spirits. (*1Corinthians 6:16,17.*)

(8)   Destruction of ministry. (*Judges 14-16.*)

(9)   Loss of integrity. (*Proverbs 6:33.*)

(10) Death. (*Proverbs 7:26,27.*)

Unfortunately, our world is all too familiar with these irrefutable consequences. But if people understand the crippling effect of sexual immorality; the question that continue to surface is why do people fornicate? I would like to suggest four reasons:

(1) God-Without a practicing relationship with God, a person will not have the power to say no to sexual temptation. (*Galatians 5:16.*)

(2) Society- The environment of our communities, billboards, prostitution, peep shows, topless dancing, dance videos, pornography, sensuous music, all contribute to sexual perversion. (*1 Corinthians 15:33.*)

(3) Alternatives- If people are not taught how to overcome sexual temptation, people will think yielding to temptation is their only option. People need sexual education from the word of God, to understand that there is another option. (*Proverbs 7:1-5.*)

(4) Mentors- Without role models of sexual integrity, it is very easy to follow the trend; fornication is a norm. In the Bible, Joseph was a role model; He said no. (*Genesis 39:7-12.*)

I believe these are four reasons that is largely contributing to the rampage of sexual immorality

(ADVICE)

Key Problem: If you are struggling with fornication; this is an issue with lust and discipline over the body and soul (mind, emotions and will.) To overcome fornication, pray, and ask God to help you apply the following steps:

(1) Prayer- Learning to schedule daily time to talk with God. (*Matthew 26:39-41, Mark 1:35, 1 John 5:14.*)

(2) Bible Study- Learning to schedule daily time to examine, and search the word of God. (*2 Timothy 2:15, 1 Peter 2:2, Psalm 1:2,3.*)

(3) Fasting- Learning to abstain from food and/or water to receive from God. I suggest a minimum fast of 3 days (36 hours) or more, and build up by starting with a partial fast (*Daniel 10:3.*) Remember, sexual sin is a deeper problem, requiring a deeper approach, and a deeper anointing (*Matthew 17:21.*) Sexual sin awakens a beast within, fasting will help starve and put this monstrous craving back

to sleep. (*Song of Solomon 3:7.*)

(4) Obedience- Learning to hear, and immediately do the word of God. (*James 1:22, Matthew 4:1-11.*)

(5) Fellowship- Learning to commit to the sharing, and partaking of a personal relationship and intimacy with God, a local Church, Christian relationships, Church affiliations, and Christian rehabilitation programs. (*1 John 1:3, Hebrews 10:25, Acts 2:41-47.*)

(6) Service- Learning to stay occupied with spiritual work. Getting involved in a local Church, or volunteering community services. If you have struggled with this problem, remember your life was occupied with serving the devil. Get busy for Jesus. God honors faithful service (*Matthew 25:23.*) It is important to practice these steps with consistency. Real change comes only with being consistent. (*St. John 8:31,32.*)

Homosexuality

Homosexuality- is two words, "homo" (same) and sexuality (sex); therefore, it is the act of being sexually aroused or attracted to someone of the same sex. It is a man being sexually attracted to another man, or a woman being sexually attracted to another woman. This act also has various expressions:

(a) lesbianism- the act of women having sex with one another,

(b) Bisexuality- the act of being sexually attracted to both sexes,

(c) Homosexual Prostitution- the act of having sex with the same gender for money,

(d) Homosexual Orientation- it is not the act of homosexual

behavior but the thoughts and imaginations of homosexual activity. In (*Matthew 5:28*), Jesus taught that a person's mind can place them into sexual sin.

(e) Effeminate- is not homosexuality, but is the act of a male who has feminine ways or behavior. It is important to understand that being effeminate is not harmless. Effeminacy has the nature of homosexuality. Like homosexuality, it distorts sexuality, and displays an imbalance of the male image.

Homosexuality is clearly a sin, based upon the word of God (*Leviticus 18:22, 20:13, Romans 1:26-32, 1 Corinthians 6:9.*) It is an activity that opposes God's plan for relationships. Homosexuality is not a pure relationship. It has no comparison to the healthy relationships that are encouraged in the word of God. In God, women are told to love women, and men are told to love men. An example of this type of love is found in (*1 Samuel 20:17*), where the scripture teaches that "*Jonathan loved David as he did his own soul.*" It was a deep love. The way God loves man. A deep unconditional love, not an impure love (*St. John 3:16.*) Moreover, (*1 Thessalonians 5:26*), says, "*greet the brethren with a holy kiss.*" It is important to note, the women kissed the women and the men kissed the men. They kissed one another on the cheek or neck (*Genesis 33:4., Acts 20:37*) However, it was nonsexual.

Because, the scriptures identify this act as an abomination before God, this would rule out the common myth, that homosexuality is a behavior or condition that one is born with. In each scripture reference to homosexuality, this sin is seen as a willful practice. This says that homosexuality requires a choice. Which means that people are not born homosexuals, they become homosexuals through choosing not to receive the help of the Holy Spirit, and the word of God. Sin is a choice (*James 1:12-14.*) Even, if you have been afflicted by the Devil with a generational curse (Exodus

20:5) and have had this sin come into your life through the blood line; in (*Galatians 3:13,14*), Jesus Christ became our curse, and cursed the curse. Therefore, when these homosexual tendencies rise up against you, by making a choice to accept Jesus Christ as Lord over your heart, and Lord over your behavior, homosexuality will never have rule over you.

In "*Encyclopedia of unusual sex and practices*" Brenda Love writes the following reasons why many have turned to homosexuality:

(a) Traumatized by someone of the opposite sex

(b) More common interest with the same sex

(c) Sex is considered more physical and passionate with the same sex

(d) The relationship can be more nurturing, and foreplay extended with the same sex

However, the major problem with homosexuality, is that it presents three serious obstacles for healthy relationships.

First, it goes against God's divine order for relationships. (*Genesis 1:27*), says, "*God created male and female*". God did not place a male with a male or a female with a female, because that was never His intended order for healthy relationships.

Second, it goes against the image of God. (*Genesis 1:27*), says, "*God created them in His image.*" Together, the male and female present the complete image of God. The man has traits that the woman does not have, and the woman has traits that the man does not have. God placed his nature in two different places; the male and female (God created them in His image.) Only the male and female together, present the complete image of God. Never, the male and male, or female and female. Male with male or female

77

with female is merely a mirror or cloning of one another; not a joining or union which God has ordained for a man and a woman as joint representatives of the full image of God. Third, it limits God's intended scope for relationships; God intended the man and woman to bear children (*Genesis 1:28.*) Because man was created to have the "image of God" (Genesis *1:26*), having children would be a promotion of the image or Glory of God. Two people of the same sex cannot have a child. Subsequently, this hinders our God-given responsibility to spread the Glory of God. Furthermore, according to (*Genesis 2:18*), God intended man to have a suitable helper, meaning a helper who would fit the overall purpose of God. The helper in Genesis 2:18, was a person of the opposite sex, not same sex. Thus, a homosexual relationship limits a person from being the suitable helper that God ordained for the marital relationship. Therefore, homosexuality is a serious problem to the plan of God.

(ADVICE)

Key Problem: If you are struggling with homosexuality; this is an issue with abuse, low self-esteem and nurture. Somewhere in your past you were either abused through the blood line (history of homosexuality in the family) or child molestation, or vulnerable acquaintance (abused by someone you trusted), resulting in the distortion of your sexuality. Furthermore, the opportunity to be nurtured by healthy role-models was more than likely absent from your childhood. The age-old question that continues to surface is, can homosexuals change? The word of God says homosexuals can change. In fact, the word of God gives a reference in (*1 Corinthians 6:9-11*), where homosexuals did change by the power of God; the scripture says, *do not be deceived. Neither fornicators, nor idolaters, nor adulterers, nor effeminate, nor homosexuals, shall inherit the kingdom of God.* In verse 11, the word says, *"and such were some of you, but you were washed, but you were sanctified, but you were justified in the name of the Lord Jesus and by the Spirit of our God.*" Notice that in the list of sinful practices was homosexuals (v10), but verse 11 says, "were" (past tense.) In other words, there were Christians at Corinth who were living in a homosexual lifestyle, but by the power of God were set free.

Everything that you are searching for in the same sex is inside of your heterosexual soulmate. Remember, (*Genesis 1:27*), "*He created him, male and female.*" God created a man with the capacity to totally satisfy a woman. To overcome homosexuality, pray, and ask God to help you apply the following steps:

1. Repent- Turn away from this sin and ask God to forgive you. (*Acts 3:19.*)

2. Separate from homosexual relationships. (*2 Corinthians 6:17,*)

3. Avoid people or things that promote sexual imbalance. (Hebrews 12:1,2,)

4. Change your lifestyle (dressing, talking, walking etc.) (*Acts 3:19,*)

5. Church- Join a Bible teaching/living Church. Allow God to nourish you through spiritual parents (Pastors) who will speak and deposit positive things into your life. (*1 Corinthians 4:15.*)

6. Ministry Group- Join a men's/women's ministry. Let God teach you how to have healthy relationships. (*Hebrews 10:25.*)

7. Word Study- Take a Bible and a Strong's Concordance and look up as many references as you can on male, female and love (God's.) For additional help, and information See Abuse, Fornication

Incest

Incest- sexual activity by people who are related by blood or marriage (*Leviticus 18:7-15.*) The arena of the family carries the highest percentage of sexual abuse. It is where people foster trust and build solid relationships. Because there is an established acquaintance.

In (*Genesis 19:31-38*), the Bible records incestuous activity between Lot and his two daughters. According to Victoria Johnson, in her book "Restoring Broken Vessels" there are three important conditions that can lead to an incestuous experience:

(1) Tragedy in the family past- Lot's father (Haran), and grandfather (Terah) dies (Genesis 11:26-32.) Tragedy can make one prone to tragedy.

(2) A family that is ignored-The scriptures do not say much about Lot's relationship with God. Whenever you ignore God you acknowledge the Devil.

(3) Hopelessness- Lot's two daughters felt because there were not available men to marry, and their father was growing past child producing years, that they were hopeless. Their hopelessness created perverted ideas, that resulted in destructive behavior.

If these three conditions exist, a family can be vulnerable to the spirit of incest. Tragedy, rejection of God, and a sense of no hope causes people to draw towards people for support. And taking God out of the picture, places Satan into the picture. (*St. John 10:10*) teaches, the devil comes to do three things: kill, steal, and destroy. Therefore, in a condition for such "neediness" people can bond in an unhealthy way. Moreover, families are not the only places prone to incest. Even, Churches can become a victim to incest. Pastors are spiritual fathers and mothers, and members are spiritual children (*1Corinthians 4:15,16, 1 John 2:1,18,28, Ephesians 4:11,12.*) If a spiritual leader allows his or her interest in membership, to move beyond spiritual guidance to that of sexual interest; the leader is guilty of incest. Although it is spiritual and not physical. It is the same dynamics, and same "spirit" (family being sexually aroused by family.)

(ADVICE)

Key Problem: If you are struggling with incest; this is an issue with abuse, and boundaries. People experiencing this type of problem have failed to set healthy limitations with family members, usually due to a history of being abused. To overcome incest, pray, and ask God to help you apply the following steps:

First, I would like to share some steps with you from *"Restoring Broken Vessels"* by Victoria L. Johnson, if you are a victim of incest:

(a) Pray

(b) Seek counsel

(c) Report the abuse to the authorities

(d) Talk to the child (if apply)

(e) Talk to the person you believe to be the abuser

(f) Gather as much information on the subject as you possibly can

I would like to share the following steps to help prevent incest:

(1) Set Boundaries- Teach your children about sex. Teach them about their body parts. Let them know where they can be touched, and not touched. The danger of being touched by strangers. Let them know that there is a time to stop bathing with parents, to stop sleeping in the same bed with parents, that there is an age to close the door when they are undressing, or using the restroom, that there is a time to dress more covered and less exposed around the home. *(Proverbs 22:5,6, Deuteronomy 6:7,8.)*

(2) Distinguish Sexes- Let your children know that there is a difference between male and female. Treat them different. This will help reinforce limitations in the life of the child. (Genesis 1:26)

(3) Healthy Affection -Display healthy feelings towards your children. Give your children hugs and kisses. Let them see affectionate behavior between mom and dad. Identify inappropriate affections, and destructive behavior. This will build emotional security and self-worth. (Ephesians *6:4, Proverbs 22:5,6.*)

(4) Communicate Openly- Communicate honestly and transparently with your children. This will keep the door of exposure open. A child is likely to talk with their parents about secrets when there is an open relationship. (*Proverbs 7:1-5.*)

(5) Authority- When ever power goes unchecked, and parents do not show accountability unto God, it can send the message that parents are above the law and what ever they do is right. This is what causes children to fill hopeless in correcting abuse, and therefore, remain a victim of abuse.

(Abuser):

1. Repent- Turn away from this sin and ask God to forgive you. (*Acts 3:19.*)

2. Counsel- Get professional Christian counsel. (*Proverbs 11:14*)

3. Practice steps to prevent incest.

For general signs of abuse, and additional help See Abuse

Internet Sex

Internet Sex- the act of engaging in sexual activity through Internet Computer Services. The Internet is an extremely powerful tool. It is the World Wide Web. It is the world brought to your finger tips.

It can be extremely helpful or extremely harmful. It's affect is determined by the user.

However, in spite of the neutrality of the Internet business , millions of people fall victim to sexual lust, through the vast services of the Internet. Stephen O. Walters in his book *"Overcoming Internet Addictions"* says, *"Every week, at least 10 percent of Americans (25 million people) visit cyber sites and sexual visits account for up to 60 percent of a Web site traffic."* This means most of the people in our country, have experienced sexual problems in one form or another. This is staggering information, and confirms how overwhelming, and addictive the Internet has become.

Moreover, the Internet has drawing cards. Websites use various strategies to draw people on-line: free gifts offered for trial services, free hours of unlimited service, with no strings attached, the convenience of credit card use, or in some cases no credit card required, e-mail, and a couple of clicks and you're on-line. It's that simple.

Website service is not a sin in itself. It's what can happen once you are on-line, that is the clincher. It is like a kid in a huge toy store; the sexual toys, and possibilities of ruining your life are unlimited: chat rooms are presented for non-stop communication with faceless friends; you never have to be concerned about your appearance, or whether or not you're groomed or presentable, neither do you have to look at a face to talk about some of your greatest secrets; bulletins boards to post a search, seeking to identify people of similar interest and problems; clubs to join a group of people who accept the way you are, where you would be otherwise rejected.

Moreover, Websites allow you to be anonymous; you don't have to use your name. You can be anybody you want (many sins are not committed because we fear being identified) just think, what it would be like, if you could be as sexually perverted as you wanted to, and nobody could recognize you. For some the thought of this is sexually titillating. Privacy is another commodity of the Internet. Some people prefer to use their names, especially in an on-line affair, but prefer to not deal with the general public. It is an occasion to keep their sexual interest on a very private and personal level. It is also an opportunity to avoid the streets, the clubs, bar scene etc, creating a sense of security and protection from sexual danger. For others, the Website is the great substitute. It replaces unwanted relationships, companionship, even broken marriages.

There is no end to the potential danger of the Internet sex. Dr. Robert Weiss, Clinical Director of the Sexual Recovery Institute in Los Angeles says, *"cyber sex is the crack cocaine of sexual addiction."* In short, Internet sex poses three major dangers:

(a) Addiction- The Internet can represent a sea of trouble, where one is lost in their own lust to an empty passion, only to drown in an addiction that can result in the loss of a marriage, job, health, identity, and over all control of life.

(b) Debt- Sexual sin is a multi-billion dollar business. You can easily lose a lot of money in a little time.

(c) Crime- Criminal cases are quickly developing at an alarming rate, over sex with minors. Our government is helpless in preventing under aged children and teenagers from using the Internet. You could be having an on-line affair with a minor, which becomes intercepted by a police officer. Cyber sex seeks to fill a hole, that is larger than your passion. A hole that only God can fill.

(d) Children- they are vulnerable due to the lack of parent supervision and unlimited games which has disguised pornography

(ADVICE)

Key Problem: If you are struggling with Internet Sex; this is a issue with addiction and lust

To overcome Internet sex, pray, and ask God to help you apply the following steps:

1. Repent- Turn away from this sin and ask God to forgive you. (*Acts 3:19,*)

2. Avoid Computer Use- stay away from computers during recovery. (*Hebrews 12:1,2.*)

3. Cancel Internet Service- Consider temporary cancellation of Internet services during recovery. (*Hebrews 12:1,2.*)

4. Avoid Pornography. (*Leviticus 18, 1 Thessalonians 5:22*)

5. Counsel- Get professional Christian counsel. (Proverbs *24:6.*)

For additional help and information See *Addiction* and *Fornication.*

Kissing

Kissing- the act of using the lips and/or the tongue to sexually arouse.

Kissing is an expression of love or affection. And inside the marriage this is healthy and expected. However, this behavior is listed as a potential sin, because of the sexual behavior" that is created by kissing outside of the marriage. Which is the focus of this discussion. The power of a kiss outside the marital covenant.

Why is a kiss so powerful? First, the lips were made for "romance" (*Song of Solomon 1:2.*) This makes the lips a romantic or sexual part of the body.

Second, when you use your lips on another person, you are sending a romantic message to their brain, unless you note the nonsexual intent of your kiss. For example, a kiss to the cheek, hand or forehead, and the presentation of yourself in a nonsexual manner are usually signs of a nonsexual kiss. But a kiss to the mouth of another person, or the mingling of tongues with another person is extremely sensuous. A kiss in a romantic context activates the brain for sexual intercourse. The body responds with increased blood flow to sexual parts of the body, the excretion of bodily fluids, rapid heart beats, and you know the rest. Outside the marriage a kiss sends a message of danger. (1 Corinthians *6:18.*)

Third, a kiss is a form of touching. It activates nerve endings that are directly connected to your brain, in particular the part that controls your sex drive. These three factors of a kiss (romantic in nature, sends message to the brain, soft to the touch) makes a kiss incredibly powerful.

Moreover, in (*Proverbs 7:13*), a young man fell into the terrible tragedy of sexual sin through a kiss. The adulterous woman, first kissed him, and it was downhill. The kiss set him up. Does that sound familiar? For many people, the relationship was fine until they started kissing. You were in perfect control until you allowed him one kiss. Some have gotten pregnant because of a kiss. Some got their heart broken because of a kiss.

Some fell into a soul-tie because of a kiss. And sadly, some couples are Christians who are living in spiritual bondage, because they are trying to live for God, but do not understand that kissing is designed to set the atmosphere for sex. In (*Proverbs 7:13*), she kissed him, and they had sex.

In simple terms, kissing is foreplay. It is the play that comes before the main event. Which explains why people engage in passionate kissing prior to sexual intercourse. The kiss is the set up. For many, their sexual nightmare started with a kiss.

(ADVICE)

Key Problem: If you are struggling with kissing (ungodly); this is an issue with lust and discipline. This is a matter of exercising discretion and self-control. To overcome kissing (ungodly), pray, and ask God to help you apply the following steps:

1. Repent- Turn away from the sin and ask God to forgive you. (*Acts 3:19.*)

2. Avoid kissing. (*1Corinthians 7:1.*)

3. Understand that kissing is an act of foreplay (it can lead to sex.) (*Song of Solomon 2, 4.*)

4. Sex outside of marriage is dangerous. (*1Corinthians 6:18.*)

5. Abstinence creates romantic value. (*Exodus 22:16,17.*)

For additional help and information See *Lust* and *Fornication.*

Lust

Lust- the act of desiring or longing for something that does not belong to you. I refer to lust as the hidden killer. Often times, people are looking for the visible, tangible, physical expression of passion in order for sin to be real. However, lust works from within. In (*Romans 1:24*), the scripture says, "*the (lust) of their hearts.*" Lust is a heart problem. It is a craving that starts on the inside, and may or may not have an outward expression. In other words, lust can strike without being visible to the physical eye. For example, many people feel safe or righteous, because they would never go to bed with someone else's spouse. However, because of the subtle power of lust, they may have already gone to bed with someone's spouse, over and over in their mind. In (*Matthew 5:28*), Jesus said "*whosoever looks on a woman to lust after her has committed adultery with her already in his heart.*" For, the word lust in this passage is "epithumeo" in the Greek, pronounced (ep-ee-thoo-meh-o) and it means desire. The root word to this term is "epi"; in the Greek it means above or beyond. Thus, the entire word "epithumeo" means a desire that goes above or beyond scriptural bounds. Hence, lust can strike from a distance, and connect two people who need not enter one another's presence.

Lust is an act of selfishness. This desire causes you to go after what you want. You never consider the possible damage that could come to others, behind your decision. In *(James 4:1-3,)* the scriptures teach that lust is based upon *"your pleasures" (v3.)* Furthermore, *(Titus 3:3.)* teaches that sexual lust can take on different expressions; *"divers* (various) *lust."* Someone may lust for the same sex, some for married persons, some for pornography, some for children, some topless dancers, and etc. Lust takes on different forms. And when these sexual cravings finish running their course, it leaves your life void and empty. *(James 4:2,)* says, *"you lust and do not have."*

However, lust hurts; the Apostle Paul makes the statement in (1 Timothy *6:9,)* harmful lust. This passion will always break someone's heart. There will continue to be a restless search that leads nowhere. Don't confuse love for lust. Love is always giving. Lust is always taking. Let God replace your lust with His love, which is total submission to God *(St. John 14:21.)* Only God can satisfy the human appetite. In *(Psalm 42:12)*, the Bible sums up the whole matter by saying, *"as the deer pants for the water brooks, so pants my soul for you O God"*, *"My soul thirsts for God, for the living God."*

(ADVICE)

Key Problem: If you are struggling with lust; this is an issue with desire and self-control. This is a problem with wanting things that are ungodly in nature, and learning how to set limits.

To overcome lust, pray, and ask God to help you apply the following steps:

1. Repent- Turn away from this sin and ask God to forgive you. (*Acts 3:19.*)

2. Avoid any practice with sexual immorality. (*1 Thessalonians 4:3.*)

3. Set limits- Practice saying "no" to sexual sin. (Genesis *39:7-12.*)

4. Guard your eyes- Avoid pornography, TV (sexual themes.)   (1 Thessalonians *5:22,*)

5. Guard your ears- Avoid sensuous music, and sensuous words. (*Ephesians 4:29, Mark 4:24,*)

6. Build a relationship with God- Learn to desire God. Ask Jesus Christ to become your Lord and Savior. Build your desire for Him, by studying and applying the word of God daily. (*1Peter 2:1, James 4:8.*)

For additional help and information See *Fornication.*

Masturbation

Masturbation- This is a very controversial subject. However, I will seek to be objective in perspective, but scriptural in content. According to one survey, 95 percent of men and 75 percent of women masturbate or have masturbated. And that at least 150,000 people in the U.S. are masturbating at any one time.

 Contrary to popular belief, there are two kinds of masturbation: (1) Mutual masturbation- this is two or more people stimulating one another's genitals to achieve sexual pleasure.

(2) Self-Masturbation- This is one stimulating their own genital to achieve sexual pleasure.

Many married couples practice the touching, and fondling of one another's genitals during sexual activity all the time. This is a form of mutual masturbation. But, this type is harmless inside the realm of marriage. Remember, sex and marriage were made for one another (*Hebrews 13:4.*)

However, I would like to focus on self-masturbation. This is the type of genital stimulation that is at the center of this discussion. I've heard many myths about masturbation:

First, that masturbation is not really sex. But, you are touching your sex organ (genitalia.) This makes the act sexual.

Second, that masturbation is healthy. It eliminates unhealthy pressure that could build up, resulting in health issues.

Third, that it is the perfect substitute for unsafe sex. You can't catch a disease, and you are not dependent upon another person for sexual satisfaction. Yes, all three of these beliefs are myths and have no scriptural foundation.

Moreover, another interesting misconception, is the interpretation of (*Genesis 38:8,9.*) Many believe that Onan was in sin, because he released his seed (sperm) on to the ground. He was asked to marry his deceased brother's wife (Tamar) according to the Mosiac Law (*Deuteronomy 25:5*), their was what was called "t*he law of marriage.*" This law taught that if a married man died, his brother (next oldest) was expected to marry the surviving wife. Onan's sin had nothing to do with masturbation, it was his rebellion to the law of God. He refused marriage, and he refused fatherhood. This was the sin.

I would to like to present four solid reasons why masturbation is both an unhealthy and unquestionable act of sin.

First, it is self-sex. God never created sex for an "individual." Sex was always designed for a couple. In (*Genesis 1:28*), the scripture says "*then God blessed them and God said to them Be fruitful and multiply"*. Notice the emphasis on them not him, not her but them. Furthermore, in *(Matthew 19:5)*, Jesus said *"and the two shall become one flesh."* Jesus confirms that sex was ordained for a "couple", not an individual.

Second, it dishonors the body. Because the body was not created for self pleasure (sexually), masturbation is an improper activity of the body . God is interested in our bodies *(Romans 12:1.)* In *(2 Corinthians 6:16)*, the scripture calls the believer's (Christian's) body "the temple of God." The temple was a sacred (holy) dwelling place.

God desires to live inside, making our bodies a "holy habitation." Anything that we do with our bodies, that does not glorify (exalt) God is a sin.

Third, it is a corrupt use of the mind. Masturbation involves the imagination. In *(2 Corinthians 10:5,)* the scripture says *"casting down imaginations and every high thing that exalts itself against the knowledge of God, and bringing into captivity every thought to the obedience of Christ."* God expects us to keep evil thoughts out of our mind. In *(Philippians 2:5,)* the scripture says, *"let this mind be in you, which was also in Christ Jesus."* Ask yourself the question, would Christ think of nude women? We are expected to think the same way God thinks.

Fourth, it is the mismanagement of emotions. Masturbation not only feels good to the body, but it makes one feel good on the inside. One, feels a sense of release and pleasure upon reaching a climax. However, it is a false satisfaction. It trains one to rely upon self-gratification, as a cure-all for getting through tempting times and stressful moments.

Masturbation teaches you to rely upon you. *(Proverbs 3:4,5,)* says, *"Trust in the Lord with all your heart, lean not to your own understanding. In all your ways acknowledge Him, and He will direct your path."* Practice turning to God, when you get a sexual urge, and God will teach you how to steer clear of your temptation.

(ADVICE)

Key Problem: If you are struggling with masturbation; this is an issue with self-centeredness. This is about relying on self-pleasure to satisfy personal needs. To overcome masturbation, pray, and ask God to help you apply the following steps:

1. Repent- Turn away from this sin and ask God to forgive you. (*Acts 3:19.*)

2. Abstinence- Avoid sex. This will teach you to trust God and not sexual gratification. (*1 Thessalonians 4:3,*)

3. Guard your mind- Avoid any material, images, words, or activity that creates sexual desire. Immediately refuse to entertain these things, it will train your mind to think like God. (*Philippians 4:8.*)

4. Honor your body- Remember, God wants your body. Avoid things that God has not ordained for your body. (*2 Corinthians 6:16.*)

5. Give the word first place- Learn to apply the Bible in everything that you do. This teaches you to trust God, not you. (*Colossians 3:17.*)

6. Word Study- Take a Bible and a Strong's Concordance and look up as many references as you can on trust, believe, and faith. For additional help and information See *Fornication* and *Lust*

Mistress

Mistress- the woman who is in a relationship with a married man.

In the Old Testament men took second wives who were called

"concubines." A concubine was a secondary-wife. She was given marital privileges, but treated with the status of a slave. She was no more than the other woman. (Judges *19:1-3, Genesis 16:1-4, Genesis 29:30.*)

It is important to note, that although this was a common practice in the Old Testament. It did not mean that it was accepted by God. (*Genesis 2:24*), clearly teaches that "*a man should be joined to his wife,*" not wives. God promoted monogamy not polygamy. Nevertheless, the other woman will never be treated with "first class" love.

Out of my 23 years of ministry, I have never seen a married man have a successful relationship with a mistress. It is a reason why this man will not let go of his wife and children.

God's blessing is on the marital covenant. His judgment is on the life of adultery (*Hebrews 13:4.*) When a man chooses a mistress, it reflects a void in his own heart. Some men view a mistress as a fantasy. An opportunity to live in two worlds. Or perhaps a back up plan. "The marriage is kind of shaky, so just in case my wife acts up." Some men see the mistress as a filler. She fills in, where my wife lacks. He says, "my wife has gained weight, she barely cooks, she doesn't compliment me, and the sex is not the same."

Whatever moves a man outside of his marriage into the arms of another women, does not reveal a problematic marriage as much as a personal emptiness in the man's own heart. There is personal trouble that only God can fix. (*Isaiah 61:1.*)

God revealed to me, when I had a lot of personal problems in my own marriage, that my wife was sweet., but I, was the sour one. The Spirit of God took me to (*Luke 6:38,*) which says, "*give and it shall be given.*" God lifted the word it from the text. He said, relationships are based upon giving. Many use this passage to talk about money, which is okay.

But, there is a bigger application. The principle of giving. God said give and it; I asked God, what did He mean? God said to me, if you give money, "it" (money) will be given back. If you give kindness it (kindness) will be given back. In other words, whatever you have gotten in your life, was first given by you. If you don't like what you have, change what you are giving. I had a lot of personal issues, and blamed my wife.

What ever I wanted to see in my wife, I started first giving to her. I changed my attitude, she changed hers. I invested more interest in my wife, she started showing more interest in my needs, and I returned as King of the Hill. When I gave to the marriage, God moved upon my wife to give to the marriage. Now, that my wife had everything that I was going into the streets to get. There were no more "excuses" for me to go to the street. Everything I needed in a woman was right in my wife, and some. Hallelujah. Thank God. Because of this revelation on giving my wife and I are happily married, and incredible partners in the ministry. God never intended two people to share another person. (*1Corinthians 7:2*), says, "*Let each man have his own wife.*"

Married man, go back to your wife, and watch God bless you. Mistress, let go and believe God for your own husband. You are valuable; God became a man, and died for you. You are very special. So special that God would offer his life for you (*1 John 3:16.*) If God will give you the greatest gift (life), would He not give you the lesser gift (your own man.)

(ADVICE)

Key Problem: If you are struggling with the mistress life; this an issue with loyalty, low self-esteem and nurture. Both parties have failed to understand commitment. Both parties more than likely came from families that did not consist of strong relationships. Relationships that did not nourish and develop marital values. To overcome the mistress life, pray, and ask God to help you apply the following steps:

1. Repent- Turn away from this sin and ask God to forgive you. (*Acts 3:19.*)

2. Break off the affair. (*Hebrews 13:4, 2 Corinthians 6:17.*)

3. Associate with strong marriages. 1 Corinthians 15:33

4. Church- Join a Bible teaching/living church. Let God nourish you through spiritual parents (Pastors) who will "speak" and "deposit" positive things into your life. (*1 Corinthians 4:15, Hebrews 10:25.*)

5. Ministry Groups- Join a men's/women's ministry. Let God teach you how to have healthy relationships. (*Hebrews 10:25.*)

6. Word Study- Take a Bible and a Strong's Concordance and look up as many references as you can on honor, and love (God's.) For additional help and information See *Adultery* and *Fornication.*

Necrophilia

Necrophilia- the act of being sexually aroused by the dead. In (*Leviticus 20:1-6,*) the Bible teaches that necrophilia is a sin. In verse 6, the Bible speaks of mediums and familiar spirits. This was an activity that involved attempts to contact the dead. The word prostitute in this passage not only speaks to the figurative use of the word referring to spiritual unfaithfulness, but there is a literal use of the term prostitute because of the term "Molech." Molech was a false deity that was always associated with sexual activity. That makes the context in this passage sexual in nature.

Because this is a sexual passage, and the scriptures speaks of the practice with familiar spirits and medium, and that the text combines sex (prostitute) with the dead (mediums and familiar spirits), this is without question a warning against an attraction to the realm of the dead with sexual arousal.

However, there is ironically, a growing popularity with necrophilia. Anything from websites, clubs, records to t-shirts are a part of this infamous trend. It is an appeal to a population that is trying to fill a spiritual void with a sexual passion for death. In the word of God, sex is considered a blessing, *"And God blessed them, and God said unto them, Be fruitful, and multiply."* But, death is never referred to as a blessing in the word of God, as it relates to the context of our discussion. Nevertheless, lets take a deeper look at the nature of death.

In scripture, death was generally referred to as a bad experience. Throughout the Old Testament death was considered a defilement, and curse *(Numbers 19:14-22, Deuteronomy 28:15.)* *(1Corinthians 15:26)*, calls death an enemy. Hence, Death was viewed as an unfortunate, and ugly experience.

Furthermore, the Bible teaches, that God is the giver of life *(Genesis 2:7.)* Therefore, death and anything associated with death would be in conflict with the very nature of God. The sexual intentions of God are clearly seen in *(Genesis 1:28)*, where the scripture says, *"And God blessed them, and God said be fruitful (sexual) and multiply."*

You cannot give instructions to a dead person. The dead cannot hear, or respond. The fact that God gave instructions, indicated that he was speaking to living beings. Subsequently, this would mean that sex was clearly designed for activity between two life-beings, not a living being and the dead. If you are a victim to this type of sexual arousal, I want to give you a general understanding of the source.

When someone has an unhealthy attraction towards the dead. This type of interest is often times traced back to the loss of a love one (spouse, parent, child, friend.) The result of death can make a person sensitive to death.

Sensitive to the point that similar emotions (pleasure, anger, fear, contentment) which are experienced during death, and experienced during sex are connected by the necrophiliac.

As strange as this may sound, emotions can become an aphrodisiac. Some people are sexually aroused, when they become angry; anger stimulates them to desire rough passionate sex. Some people are sexually aroused over the fear of being caught. Or the fear of risk. Necrophilia connects death and sex through these, and other emotions. However, to a necrophiliac association with death becomes a form of nourishment. It nourishes both the emotional and sexual void. For additional help and information See *Abuse*

(ADVICE)

Key Problem: If you are struggling with necrophilia; this is an issue with loss, low self-esteem and nurture. To overcome necrophilia, pray, and ask God to help you apply the following steps:

1. Repent- Turn away from this sin and ask God to forgive you. (*Acts 3:19.*)

2. Counsel- Get professional Christian counsel. (*Proverbs 11:14*)

3. Avoid things associated with death (funeral homes, grave yards morgues, death recordings, necrophilia clubs, suicidal or homicidal thoughts.) (*Deuteronomy 30:19.*)

4. Church- Join a Bible teaching/living church. Allow God to nourish your empty heart through spiritual parents (Pastors) who will

"speak" and "deposit" positive things into your life. (*1 Corinthians 4:15.*)

5. Ministry Groups- Join a men's/women's ministry. Allow God to teach you how to build healthy relationships. Hebrews 10:25

6. Word Study- Take a Bible and a Strong's Concordance and look up as many references as you can on love (God's.)

Nudity

Nudity- the act of totally or partially removing clothing to the point of exposing private parts for sexual pleasure.

Before I go into the core of this subject I would like to discuss some common circumstances of nudity. All nudity is not inappropriate. There is what would be recognized as acceptable nudity. Such as a child whose body is exposed, when a diaper is being changed, or a child whose body is exposed when being bathed, or the exposure of a body during the preparation for burial, or exposure of a person's body during hospitalization, or an athlete whose competition, requires light clothing, leaving the athlete very exposed, or the exposure of a body that's being used for educational purposes during medical training. These circumstances of nudity are not prohibited by scripture.

However, lets look at the type of nudity that is condemned by the word of God. But, before we go into the word of God, I want to state my view on a controversial issue of nudity. This issue is about cultural nudity. This is the type of nudity that has been determined by a culture or race of people as a norm. For example, this type of nudity can be seen in the countries of Africa. Where it is normal for women to walk about topless, fully exposing their breasts, or for men to walk about only wearing a string and thin cloth that barely covers the genitals.

I believe cultural nudity is not acceptable to God. Man does not have the authority to determine spiritual law. Even though nudity may be apart of a culture, people are people, and regardless of where you may live on the face of the earth, *"All men have sinned and fallen short of the Glory of God" (Romans 3:23.)* Each human being is made of the same substance, *"a sinful nature."* Furthermore, each person must deal with the Lust of the eyes (1 John *2:15,16.*) This is the make-up of all men, until they are converted by the Lord Jesus Christ.

Thus, nudity could never be designed for any culture, race or group of people. However, in (*Leviticus 18*), the scriptures teach that nudity with evil intention or consequences is prohibited by scripture. Moreover, (*Genesis 9:20-25,*) records Noah's son (Ham) looking upon his father's naked body with evil intention.

This is the kind of nudity that is at the core of the sex industry, which is a multi-billion dollar business. And the issue that stands above this shocking news is that these dollars represent the multitudes (millions) of people who have become sexual victims to the appearance of a nude body.

Our society has unfortunately provided no cushion against this social blight. We are bombarded with pictures through various channels: TV, billboards, videos, magazines, scantly dressers, nude beaches, nude marathons, nude artists

Our so called watchdogs (Censorship Authorities) who were organized to protect the citizens of our country from the presentation of inappropriate material, have progressively lowered their standards for determining safe material, and categorizing material for the audience appropriate for that material.

Furthermore, our community has placed nudity into hard and soft categories: full nudity and partial nudity. It is said that, full nudity is for adults only, and partial nudity is safe for children while under parental guidance. Yes, this is as contradicting as it sounds. Nudity that is sexual in nature, is nudity whether in full or part. For example, how much poison would you need to eat to become poisoned? Whether you took a lot or a little you would be poisoned. Nudity is dangerous to any degree, and hazardous to your health.

However, we must also understand that sexual sin is progressive (Romans 1:22-27.) You may start with the peeping of bare breasts, or the glance of a raised skirt. But, this will soon graduate into a passion for more. It is a scriptural law of increase or "*sowing and reaping*" (Galatians 6:7,8.)

Whatever you do, you produce the ability to do it again, and again, to where again is not enough. Now, the sexual craving takes you beyond repetition into volume. Now, you are asking for more sexual content to satisfy the same sexual desire. It's like an alcoholic who has four drinks a day. After a few months, he doesn't feel a high or buzz. So, he starts taking six drinks a day, and the high returns. The alcoholic has to take in more liquor just to get the same high. Nudity will take you on the same trip. The trick of the devil is to start you small. Because, small has an appearance of innocence.

Before you know it, you're in the big house (big time trouble.) This is why our children are developing sexual vocabularies, and behavioral patterns that we did not teach them. This is why young girls are getting pregnant at 13 years of age, and young boys are viewing girls as trophies of sexual conquest. Where is this coming from? Heavy exposure to nudity, and sexual perversion. It's time to expose our families to the word of God. Sexual education is in order. Tell your family what God has to say about sex. King Solomon taught his son in (*Proverbs 7:1-5.*) Lets put nudity in it's proper place. And the only place for sexual nudity, is marriage. In (*Genesis 2:25,*) the scripture says "*they were both naked, the man and his wife, and were not ashamed.*"

(ADVICE)

Key Problem: If you are struggling with nudity; this is an issue with dishonor. Nudity outside of the marriage is about lacking the honor and value for the sexuality of one's body. To overcome nudity, pray, and ask God to help you apply the following steps:

1. Repent- Turn away from this sin and ask God to forgive you. (*Acts 3:19.*)

2. Avoid any pornographic material. (*1 Thessalonians 5:22, Leviticus 18.*)

3. Avoid any activity that promotes nudity. (*Hebrews 12:1,2.*)

4. Mentors- Hang around people who have set sexual standards. (*2 Timothy 2:22.*)

5. Word Study- Take a Bible and a Strong's Concordance and look up as many references as you can on the body, and honor. For additional help and information See *Lust* and *Fornication*

Oral Sex

Oral Sex- the act of being sexually aroused by touching the genitalia with the mouth and/or tongue. I want to attempt to provide some food for thought on such a very controversial subject. I want to begin by first dividing this discussion into two types of oral sex: oral sex within the marriage, and oral sex outside the marriage.

First, oral sex outside of marriage is not the will of God. In (*1 Thessalonians 4:3*), the scripture says "*for this is the will of God, your sanctification that you should abstain from* **fornication**." Fornication is defined as any immoral or ungodly sex. Furthermore, in (*Genesis 1:28*), the scripture teaches that God said to **them**

(Adam/Eve) *"be fruitful and multiply."* God gives sexual permission to Adam and Eve, who were married (*Genesis 2:23-25.*) This says, that God intended the experience of sex to only take place in the context of marriage. Which says, that no one has a right to have sex in any form with someone they are not married to. Thus, oral sex in this context becomes sexual sin.

Moreover, there is the issue of virgins who are sexually active, but remain virgins. I know that sounds confusing, but it is a deceptive practice that's spreading like wildfire. This has become a common misconception as safe sex.

Sex outside of marriage is never safe. In (*Hebrews 13:4,*) the Bible says *"marriage is honorable among all and the bed undefiled; but fornicators and adulterers God will judge."* Sexual immorality brings the danger of divine judgment. Gynecologist, and medical doctors have documented cases where oral sex has led to gonorrhea of the mouth. Shockingly, if gonorrhea can live in the mouth, this would both explain and support why sexually transmitted diseases are rapidly spreading; oral sex. So much for safe sex.

I'm sure we remember when former President Bill Clinton was caught in one of the sex scandals of the century. He was clearly asked, "Did you have sex with Monica Lewinsky?" He replied, by saying "I did not have sex with that woman." Later, it was discovered that he performed oral sex on Ms. Lewinsky, and she on him, which in his mind was not sex.

Where did the notion that if it's not sexual intercourse or penetration, it's not sex, come from? Allow me to answer that; this lie came from Satan himself. Jesus said in (*Matthew 5:28,*) *"whoever looks at a woman to lust for her has already committed adultery with her in his heart."* A person can commit sexual sin with their mind. In (*1 Corinthians 6:19,20*) the scriptures teach, that the body of a believer is a temple or place of worship. And if God desires the body of a believer, likewise He desires that the body of one who does not know Jesus as their Lord and Savior to be kept clean and free of sexual immorality. However, oral sex encompasses the mental and physical aspects of sexual immorality, and outside of marriage is totally forbidden by God.

Second, oral sex within the marriage. It is my belief and conviction that oral sex among married couples is not a violation of God's word. I want to list three reasons, why I believe oral sex is biblically permissible in a marriage:

(1) The nature of the mouth- in the scriptures, the mouth has general uses: eating (*Ezekiel 24:17,22,*) communication (*Hebrews 13:15, Proverbs 24:2,*) romance (*Song of Solomon 1:2, 4:3,*) Lets us highlight it's romantic use, which brings us to the opposing view that states oral sex is unnatural.

How do we determine what is natural or unnatural. You must identify the original design or purpose of a given thing. For example, anal sex is unnatural because the anus was designed to release waste. Many use the anus for sexual pleasure, but fail to see it has no sexual purpose.

However, I want to note that the entire body, with the exception of the areas designed for non-sexual use, can become an erogenous zone (sexually sensitive.) King Solomon validates this fact as he details the body of his bride with words of passion. (*Song of Solomon 7:1-9, 4:1-6.*) I made this point, because I am aware that a sensitive touch anywhere on the body can be sexually arousing. However, I caution you to remember the law of moderation. There must be a limit to anything. In order to have a healthy sex-life there must be limitation and self control. (*1 Corintians 7:5,9.*)

Nevertheless, because the mouth has a sexual purpose, and the vagina or penis has sexual purpose; it is my conviction that inside the covenant of marriage, because of the joining of two purposes similar in nature, oral sex in moderation is scripturally sound.

(2) Agreement- sex is a consensual experience. A couple should always "agree" with one another to have sex or not have sex. No one should be forced to have oral sex, or made to feel guilty for desiring oral sex. Each couple has a right to agree on the desired sex. In (*1 Corinthians 7:5*), the scripture says, "*Do not deprive one another except with consent for a time that you may give yourselves to fasting and prayer, and come together again so that Satan does not tempt you because of your lack of self-control.*"

Notice the word consent. This says that God never intended for sex to be "forceful", and that if sex between a couple is agreeable within moderation, it is acceptable before God.

(3) Conscience- Any sexual activity that conflicts with your conscience should be avoided (*Romans 14:23.*) But, if a couple is clear in their conscience about a sexual activity in moderation it is acceptable before God (*Romans 2:15.*) I believe the nature of the mouth, agreement, and conscious, are three scriptural grounds for oral sex.

However, remember, oral sex outside of the marriage is clearly a sin, but inside the marriage, I believe it is acceptable unto God.

(ADVICE)

Key Problem: If you are facing oral sex difficulties; this is an issue with preference, If you prefer oral sex or do not prefer oral sex; one choice is not better than the other . It is strictly matter of preference. To overcome oral sex difficulties, pray, and ask God to help you consider the following steps:

Outside the marriage:

1. Repent- Turn away from this sin and ask God to forgive you.

(*Acts 3:19.*)

2. Avoid sex. (*1 Thessalonians 4:3.*)

Inside the marriage:

(1) Follow your conscience. (*Romans 2:14,15.*)

(2) Mutual Agree. (*1 Corinthians 7:5.*)

(3) Understand the nature of the "mouth." (*Song of Solomon 1:2.*)

For additional help and information Fee *fornication*, *Lust* and *Adultery*

Object Sex

Object Sex- the act of having sex with objects. There are two ways to look at the subject of object sex. First, you can have sex involving objects such as: lingerie, which is very appealing to the eyes, music (a tape or CD), which can add relaxation to the atmosphere, food which can create a social affect and opportunities to be creative, turning him or her into a meal; oils, which can be very soothing, or scents (cologne, perfume, incense) smelling good can be a real turn on. These are some of the types of objects or fetishes used during sex which are harmless.

However, second, is sex with an object itself. This could involve sex with a toy sex-doll, sex with a teddy bear, a mattress (something soft and filling; similar to the touch of a human body), or in many cases a snake. In the middle East, and many religious cults, sex with snakes are a popular ritual.

Cross-dressing is probably the most common form of object sex. The feeling of certain clothing (slips, dresses, stockings, high heels) can feel good to the skin, or appeal to a feminine side of a man, and thus be arousing. Then there is the rising demand for elaborate sex machines that look like something out of a wielding shop, designed to duplicate any sexual behavior performed by a human being. And then last but not least, there is people although people are not objects within the context of this discussion, but because many are extremely self-centered on their pursuit of sexual passion, they treat people as mere objects of sex...nothing less and nothing more.

However, sex to or with an object is prohibited by the word of God. According to (*Genesis 1:28*), "*And God blessed them, and God said be fruitful (*sexual*) and multiply.*" Sex was designed for "them" or people. In this passage we clearly see the intended participants of sex: people, not objects. God never intended people to have sex with objects. (that is to an object.)

(ADVICE)

Key Problem: If you are struggling with object sex; this is an issue with isolation, low self-esteem and abuse. Most people who have a sexual attraction for objects are anti-sociable in nature. Generally, they do not interact much with people, due to a history of abuse.

To overcome object sex, pray, and ask God to help you apply the following steps:

1. Repent- Turn away from this sin and ask God to forgive you. (*Acts 3:19.*)

2. Church- Join a Bible teaching/living church. Let God nourish you through spiritual parents (Pastors) who will "*speak*" and "*deposit*" positive things into your life. (*1 Corinthians 4:15, Hebrews 10:25.*)

3. Group Ministry- Join a men's/women's fellowship. Allow God to teach you how to build healthy relationships. (*Hebrews 10:25.*)

4. Avoid sexual attraction toward objects- (*Exodus 20:3,4.*)

5. Word Study- Take a Bible and a Strong's Concordance and look up as many references as you can on love (God's.)

For additional help and information See *Abuse*

Orgy

Orgy- the act of engaging in group sex. Group sex goes against the nature of sex. God created sex as a private experience. An intimate experience to be shared between a husband and wife. Orgies are nothing less than sexual smorgasbords. One of the rules in a smorgasbord, is no limit or all you can eat. Whenever you remove the word of God (limit) from the human will, there is always the likelihood of going "overboard."

Because limits are removed, orgies can also be very unsafe. The chances of contracting a disease, are greatly increased. One, has to also understand that orgies are generally accompanied with drinking. Drinking impairs your judgment, causing you to make decisions you regret later. In (*Exodus 32:6*), the Bible says, "*And the people sat down to eat and drink and rose up to play.*" The word play in the Hebrew is "tsachaq" pronounced (tsaw-khak); it means to sport, foreplay or to engage in sexual play. a cross reference to this word, can be seen in (*Genesis 26:8*), where Isaac is sporting (foreplay) Rebekah.

God judged the nation of Israel for their group participation in drinking and sexual immorality. God has never promoted polygamy (multiple sex partners), but has established monogamy (one partner), as a foundational concept in marriage. (*Matthew 19:5*), declares, "*And the two, shall become one flesh.*" God made a "man" with the capacity to safely handle one woman at a time. Likewise, God made a woman with the capacity to safely handle one man at a time. Anything beyond the two-concept would be counterproductive to God's original blueprint for a successful marriage, and would never work.

To give you an example of how powerful an orgy can be to a person; (*1 Kings 11:1-3*), teaches that a powerful spiritual leader by the name of King Solomon, traded his Kingdom (ministry), his anointing (power), his integrity, his reputation, and his God, for 700 wives, and 300 concubines, totaling a thousand women for his sexual enjoyment. This was nothing compared to Solomon's entire life, and career (ministry), sacrificed for a cheap thrill and a quick feel in the game of sexual sin.

Sexual sin is very attractive, because man is naturally a sex-being (*Genesis 1:28.*) But, it's attraction can be multiplied to no end, when it is put in the setting of a "group."

(ADVICE)

Key Problem: If you are struggling with orgies; this is an issue with discipline. It is a form of addiction. It is sexual passion in excess or without restraint.

To overcome orgies, pray, and ask God to help you apply the following steps:

For steps, please see key problem under *Addiction* and *Fornication*

Pedophilia

Pedophilia- the act of an adult being sexually aroused by a child. Out of all the victims to sexual sin, children are the "victim of victims." This group includes infants, children, and teenagers.

It is also important to note that there are two other types of people, who are aroused by children: a hebephile has sexual urges for children who are older than 13 but younger than 18; a ephebophile has sexual urges for children (adolescents) older than 18. However, these two classes of sexual passion differ only in the targeted age group of their sexual attraction.

Such interest still fall into the same spirit or nature of pedophilia; sexual attraction for children, it's all the same. Children lack physical, mental, and emotional development making them vulnerable to abuse in every form, particularly sexual abuse. (*Numbers 31:18*), the scriptures teach that adults were forbidden from sexual intercourse with children. In (*1 Corinthians 7:1,2*) "*Now concerning the things of which you wrote to me: It is good for a man, not to touch a woman. Nevertheless, because of sexual immorality, let each man have his own wife, and let each woman have her own husband.*" Notice the emphasis on "*man and woman*" as God addresses sex. He speaks to a husband and wife, but also to a man and woman. In other words, God is addressing two "adults" in this context of sex. The reason being, is that sex is meant to be an adult experience.

If this is true, it would never be scripturally permissible for and adult to have sex with a child. No where in scripture is child sex permitted. Every mention of sex in it's proper context (marriage) always refer to an adult with an adult.

I want to add, one of the reasons that sex is limited to adults, besides that of marriage, is that sex is a very powerful experience. It is the ability to make (birth) another human being, and with the same ability destroy a human being physically, mentally and spiritually (*1Corinthians 6:18.*) However, a pedophile has skills that places him or her in a position to manipulate a minor into sexual intercourse:

(A) Affection is a natural and easy trait. For, the trust of a child can be easily won as an adult repeatedly displays interest, and concern. Because affection builds trust, it is important to screen babysitters, teachers, mentors or anyone working close to your children. Trust is the key that opens the door to opportunity. Most child molesters gain an abusive position by developing the child's trust. Which is not difficult, when someone shows what appears to be genuine affection.

(B) Friendship is an area that the pedophile has mastered. The adult will build a close relationship with the child, appearing to be a special buddy or unique pal. Because of the relationship and closeness that a child may share with an adult, harmful behavior can be easily disguised as a harmless gesture. The adult may ask a sexual favor, that comes across something like this; *"can you stay upstairs with me, and change your clothes, so that we can continue our conversation"* but, in actuality the adult just wants to peep at the child's body.

(C) Baiting is what the abuser will use to condition the child for sexual abuse. The adult might pick selective times to ask the child to help him or her get undressed, or the adult might undress in front of the child and ask sexual questions, or go as far as performing oral sex on the child as a means of comforting the child in moments of anxiety.

These three traits: affection, friendship, and baiting are things to watch for in the arena of the people we allow around our children.

A pedophile is most often a male, but can be a female. They come in all forms: young, old, tall, short, white, black, rich poor. It could be anybody. For signs of sexual child abuse, see *Abuse*.

(ADVICE)

Key Problem: If you are struggling with pedophilia; this is an issue with abuse and nurture. You are suffering from a broken childhood. Your fantasies, are nothing but unhealthy desires for a missing childhood. Generally, when a person has unhealthy feelings about children, there was not proper nurturing during childhood (*Ephesians 6:4.*) Remember, when an adult has sex with a child, it's nothing short of sexual abuse. The Bible declared it, the law has established it, and society despises it. Pedophilia is both a sin and a crime.

To overcome pedophilia, pray, and ask God to help you apply the following steps:

(Abuser):

1. Repent- Turn away from this sin and ask God to forgive you. (*Acts 3:19.*)

2. Avoid prolonged contact with children during the recovery period.

3. Church- Join a Bible teaching/living church. Allow God to nourish you through spiritual parents (Pastors.) (*2 Corinthians 6:17,18, 1Corinthians 4:15.*)

4. Ministry Groups- Join a men's/women's fellowship. Allow God to help you build healthy relationships. (*Hebrews 10:25.*)

5. Counsel- Get professional Christian counsel. (*Proverbs 24:5.*)

(Victim):

(1) Counsel- Get professional Christian counsel. (*Proverbs 24:5.*)

(2) Follow steps, under the subject of Abuse.

For additional help and information See *Abuse.*

Piercing

Piercing- the act of puncturing or breaking the skin to receive sexual arousal. Many people practice piercing for sexual purposes, by piercing the genitals. Which is another form of sadomasochism, which focuses on pain to achieve sexual excitement (see *Sadism.*) Piercing devalues the preciousness of the human body. In (*Leviticus 19:28*), the Bible says, "*you shall not make any cuttings*

111

in your flesh for the dead." The nation of Israel was forbidden from inflicting any physical disfigurement or bodily harm. God also challenged their motive, they were not only cutting themselves, but was doing it for the purpose of the dead. Their cutting had nothing to do with God.

However, what was the connection between cutting and piercing? They both break the skin and subject the body to injury. And in the context of sexuality, it has nothing to do with God. In (*Mark 5:1-15*), the scriptures tell of a man cutting himself with stones. Jesus delivers him from demonic possession, and states, the man was now in his *"right mind"* (*vv5,15.*) This meant that before Jesus freed the man, he was in the wrong mind. In this wrong mind the man was cutting himself. In other words, cutting and breaking the skin without a legitimate cause was connected to not being in his right mind. As far as God is concern, you are not in your right mind to cut, break or puncture your skin for sexual pleasure.

Some people have gotten their tongue, navel, eyebrows, or a full body piercing as a sexual statement. This is not the way God desires sex to be presented. Now, I am aware that people have gotten their ears pierced (earrings) or nose pierced (nose rings) and this is harmless. However, when a person breaks the skin of their body for sexual reasons, it is in conflict with God's purpose for sex. A person may pierce the skin during sex, or get a body piercing (the breasts, tongue or vaginal) to make a sexual statement. Either choice is a promotion of Sadism. It promotes an unhealthy view of sex, and is therefore, against the will of God (*Colossians 3:17,23.*)

Body piercing opposes three basics principles of scripture:

(A) Health- Piercing creates openings in the skin, making the body vulnerable to infections, not to mention the shedding of blood. Blood can carry diseases, God wants us healthy not sick. (*3 John 1:2.*)

(B) Gentleness- This is a painful expression of passion. The fruit of the Holy Spirit is gentleness. (*Galatians 5:22.*)

(C) Image- God wants your body to present the image of God. Piercing presents the sensual image of the world. (*Genesis 1:26, 1Corinthians 6:18-20.*)

Essentially, body piercing goes against the plan of God for your body.

(ADVICE)

Key Problem: If you are struggling with piercing; this is an issue with image, honor, and low self-esteem. It is an act of dishonor to puncture or use the body to promote a sexual statement, rather than the "image" of God. To overcome piercing, pray, and ask God to help you apply the following steps:

1. Repent- Turn away from this sin and ask God to forgive you. (*Acts 3:19.*)

2. Practice using the body to promote God. (*1 Corinthians 6:20.*)

3. Avoid wearing things that conflict with the word of God. (*Hebrews 12:1.*)

4. Avoid things that are physically unhealthy. (*3 John 1:2.*)

5. Church- Join a Bible teaching/living Church. Allow God to nourish you through spiritual parents (Pastors) who will speak and deposit positive things into your life. (*1 Corinthians 4:14, Hebrews 10:25.*)

6. Word Study- Take the Bible and a Strong's Concordance and look up as many references as you can on honor and body.

For additional help and information See *Sadism.*

Pimp

Pimp- a man who uses prostitutes to gain money. The lifestyle of a pimp, is not limited to men, but their are women who gain from prostitution, called madams. It is interesting to note that you can be pimped by a man or a woman. The only thing that changes, are the titles, not the activity. It's the similar and common use of prostitutes for financial gain. In (*Romans 1:27*), the scripture says, "*And likewise also the men, leaving the natural use of the woman, burned in their lust one toward another.*" Notice the phrase "*lust one toward another.*" In this passage, the term lust in the Greek is "*orexis*" pronounced (or-ex-is.) The word means, to long after something for self-use. Looking back to the passage on the phrase "*lust one toward another*"; lust has each person seeking personal satisfaction. The pimp has a sexual desire that results in self gain. It is this pursuit of self interest, that has led to two important traits of the pimp:

First, a pimp is controlling. He seeks to control the life of the prostitute through violence, which ultimately leads to fear. Many prostitutes are physically assaulted, and verbally abused. Often times drugs are given to these women to create mental imbalance, making them more susceptible to the domination of the pimp.

Second, pimps are deceptive. A pimp is an artist at manipulating words. He will get the prostitute to believe she is helpless without his aid. That she is great only because of his strengths, and resources. A pimp presents himself as a father figure, prepared to pay for her needs: rent, clothes, food, hair, nails, bail money etc. The pimp will come across as the only one, who really cares about her, and truly understands her. Control and deception are powerful tools in the hands of a pimp. However, God desires to be a Father to you, and supply all your needs with a pure love. (*2 Corinthians 6:17,18, Philippians 4:19.*) It is not the will of God, for a person to control another person. In (*Genesis 1:26*), God told man to take dominion over everything in the earth, "*except another person.*"

(ADVICE)

Key Problem: If you are struggling with the life of a pimp; this is an issue with control and deception. To overcome the life of a pimp, pray, and ask God to help you apply the following steps:

1. Repent- Turn away from this sin and ask God to forgive you. (*Acts 3:19.*)

2. Church- Join a Bible teaching/living church. Submit to godly authority. This will challenge the controlling spirit. (*Hebrews 13:7,17.*)

3. Honesty- Practice speaking truth filled words. (*Ephesians 4:25.*)

4. Word Study- Take the Bible and a Strong's Concordance and look up as many references as you can on authority, and lies.

Phone Sex

Phone Sex- the act of sexually seducing or being seduced over the phone by words. According to the St. James Encyclopedia of Pop Culture, phone sex started in the 1980s. It's core motive was an attempt to engage in safe sex. The popularity of phone sex grew rapidly over the belief that it was the perfect replacement for harmful sex: pornography, prostitution, sexual harassment, rape, incest and so on.

Phone sex became an exciting game. The fantasy-maker (one of the names or a phone sex operator) and the customer could play any role, and act out any fantasy. No identities were released, no commitments required, no diseases contracted. Which could be done through either a recorded message or a live operator. Phone sex appeared safe and harmless. But, sexual sin is "never" safe. (*Proverbs 7:21-27.*)

Statistics indicate that phone sex adds to sexual abuse against women, an increase in divorces, and rise in sex crimes. Moreover, sex operators have reported feeling abused, as men act out their fantasy by saying whatever turns them on. Many operators have reported, that the pay is low, and not nearly compatible to the abuse suffered.

Records indicate the alarming rate at which millions are going into debt, and being eaten alive of their bill money, life savings, and credit cards through the phone sex industry. This doesn't sound so safe. This is the all familiar picture of sexual sin; it reveals a big picture of pleasure, never allowing you to see that behind the same picture are the crippling consequences of sin. (Romans *6:23.*) In (*Ephesians 4:29*), the Bible says "*Let no corrupt communication proceed out of your mouth.*" In (*Mark 4:24*), the Bible says "*Take heed how you hear.*" These two verses strongly teach that God is concerned about words and what we hear.

Words are powerful; they are seeds, containing life or death (*Proverbs 18:21.*) Furthermore, hearing shapes what you believe, and what you believe is what you live by. In (*Romans 10:17,*) the Bible says, "*Faith comes by hearing and hearing by the word of God.*" The Apostle Paul was talking to the Corinthian Church on how faith is created. You continuously hear the word of God. However, God used Apostle Paul to present a more general application; hearing creates believing. In other words, whatever you hear enough, be it positive or negative, you will eventually believe.

Phone sex plants dirty words into your hearing. Dirty hearing create dirty beliefs. This begins to pervert your entire outlook on life including sex. Which brings us to the last area of application, the mind. Words create images. If I said to you, I saw a big black cat jump over a fence, you would visualize a black cat jumping over a fence. This is how the mind comprehends communication. Words are spoken and the mind visualizes it.

It is upon this principle, that sex over the phone; a multi-billion dollar industry is extremely stimulating and captivating. When a sex operator starts speaking fantasies the customer can see it, in his or her mind.

Phone sex is a game of words and images. Let God change the program, and redesign the moves.

(ADVICE)

Key Problem: If you are struggling with phone sex; this is an issue with hearing and words. It is a choice to open your hearing to dirty words, which creates dirty images leading to a dirty life. To overcome phone sex, pray, and ask God to help you apply the following steps:

1. Repent- Turn away from this sin and ask God to forgive you. (*Acts 3:19.*)

2. Guard your mind- Refuse evil thoughts. (*2 Corinthians 10:4,5, Philippians 4:8.*)

3. Avoid dirty conversations. (*Psalm 1:1, Ephesians 4:29.*)

4. Avoid people who choose to live dirty (sexually immoral.) (*2 Corinthians 6:17.*)

5. Continuously hear the word of God. (*Joshua 1:8, Colossians 3:10.*)

Player

Player- one who toys with another for sexual pleasure. In (*Judges 16:4,5*), the scripture says "*Afterward it happened that he loved a woman in the Valley of Sorek, whose name was Delilah. And the lords of the Philistines came up to her and said to her, entice him and find out where his great strength lies, and by what means we may overpower him.*"

In this classic story of sexual sin, notice verse 4, which indicates that "*Samson loved Delilah*", but the scriptures never say that she loved him. For Delilah, the pursuit of destroying Sampson was a game. She deceived him. She had no personal interest in Sampson. But Sampson driven by the passion of his own lust, was blinded to her deadly plan. The fifth verse tells us she wanted his strength (anointing.) Isn't it amazing that people can appear one way on the outside, but have a different position on the inside?

Nevertheless, reading this entire chapter, one will learn that this story had a sad ending. Samson lost his anointing, ministry, and he lost his life, due to the game of seduction.

The story of Sampson and Delilah reveals the toying aspect of sexual sin.

Sexual sin creates one big game, where the participants are called players. The game has only two rules: lying and deception. The best liar and best deceiver are the champions in the game of sexual seduction. Females are called playgirls, and males are called playboys. They are people who play with the lives of others for sexual pleasure. The player is always role-playing. This person lives behind an image that does not reflect the true person. The player lives in a soap opera that never ends.

Players can fall into various types: an adulterer plays with marriages or sexual pleasure; a prostitute plays with sexual favors for money; an erotic dancer plays with enticing motions of the body for money; he exhibitionist plays with the act of exposing sexual images of hemselves to the public; the flirt (philanderer) plays with the idea of sexually arousing someone with no serious intent; the cheater plays with the thrill of multiple relationships outside of a serious relationship, and the list goes on. However, they all play, and life tself becomes a game. Nevertheless, a person who plays is generally a victim of a generational curse.

n (*Exodus 20:5*), the scriptures speak of the "*sins of the fathers, being passed down from one generation to another.*" The simple meaning of this passage is that the "*ungodly actions*" of the parents are transferred to the children through the bloodline. The blood contains DNA which carries information. This information contains habits and behavior. This is why you will here somebody say "*boy you remind me of your daddy or girl your momma was the same way.*" Or have you ever seen a family of alcoholics. How did that happen? The "*law of generation*" found in (*Matthew 7:17*), which says "*But a bad tree bears bad fruit.*" A bad source will produce bad consequences. If a parent (tree) has a corrupt heart, this will pass down into their fruit (children), subsequently, becoming victims of the generational curse. Nevertheless, every game comes to an end. One day, the law of reciprocity catches up with the player. This is the law of sowing and reaping. It finally happens the player gets played. You cannot continue sowing games, and games do not come back.

(ADVICE)

Key Problem: If you are struggling with the life of a player this is an issue with commitment and honesty.

To overcome the life of the player, pray, and ask God to help you apply the following steps:

1. Repent- Turn away from this sin and ask God to forgive you (*Acts 3:19.*)

2. Practice telling the truth. (*Ephesians 4:25.*)

3. Keep your word. (*Matthew 5:37.*)

4. Commit to building healthy relationships (people in general. (Matthew 22:39.)

5. Word Study- Take a Bible and a Strong's Concordance and look up as many references as you can on faithful and lies.

Pornography

Pornography- any material (printed or video) that has been designed to create sexual arousal. Pornography is a multi-billion dolla industry. When ever this much money is being spent, it means tha millions upon millions of people are receiving the services. Which means, a lot of people are victims of sexual arousal by visua stimulation.

Even the church has shockingly, fallen within these statistics. The National Federation for Decency Journal reported that Penthouse Magazine claims, *"that 35% of it's readers are born again Christians, and that those numbers translates into 1.67 million Christian readers."*

In *"Encyclopedia of Unusual Sex Practices"*, Brenda Love states that *"Pornography in its original meaning porne (prostitute) and graphos (to write), meant a writing about prostitutes, but was later broadened to any material designed to sexually aroused."* If you stop and think about it, pornography contains women who expose their bodies for money. This is basically what prostitutes do.

Moreover, Dr. Patrick Carnes in *"Don't call it Love, Recovery from Sexual Addiction"* states, that *"pornography is one of the building blocks to sexual addiction."* In other words, pornography is such a powerful tool in the hand of the Devil, that if you are frequently involved in pornography, it is likely that you will become a sexual addict.

Pornography manipulates one of man's most influential areas in life, the eyes. In (*1 John 2:16*), the scripture says *"for all that is in the world, the lust of the flesh, the pride of life, and the lust of the eyes."* Satan has only three channels, through which he enters the human life: the lust of the flesh, the pride of life, and *"lust of the eyes."* It was through the *eyes* that the Devil deceived Eve out of her inheritance (Garden of Eden.) In (*Genesis 3:6*), the scripture says, *"so when the woman saw that the tree was good for food."* For, it's been said that "a picture is worth a thousand words". What the mind sees through the eyes can say a lot to the soul.

In all learning institutions visual aids are always used. Teachers understand that it is a proven fact, that if you can "show" someone what you are verbally communicating, it has a much more effective influence on the brain than words alone. Nevertheless, I wanted to present some examples about the eyes to demonstrate how powerful the visual arena of life can be to the human mind. Which, Satan understands this principle all too well.

This is why pornography has not only a stimulating affect, but a lingering influence upon the mind. A person can pick up a porn magazine or view a porn video tape, and have a hard time staying away from the material. Even, one week or one month or several years after he or she has seen the pictures, the images are subtly and deeply embedded into the soul. Pornography saturates your mind, emotions and will.

In (*2 Samuel 11*), King David stared at a beautiful naked woman by the name of Bathsheba, as she bathed herself. This experience was pornographic in nature. Lust filled King David's eye's which resulted in adultery with Bathsheba and the schemish killing of her husband. A biblical account of fatal attraction. What happen? Watching a naked women overwhelmed his soul. This is what pornography is all about, observation of the nude.

Watching television as a form of relaxation or family entertainment several years ago was a healthy and innocent use of free time. But nowadays, in an attempt to eat the meat we can easily choke on the bones. TV is filled a lot of good, but the bad is so much greater that it is difficult to watch TV for an extended period of time, and not become affected in a negative way.

According to *"Nielsen Media Research"* the average U.S. household watches approximately 8 hours of television a day or 56 hours a week.

This is a lot of exposure to the overwhelming images of TV. Because sex sells, and boosts ratings, this would explain why most of television programming is sexual in theme and content, and why the world has gone *"sex crazy."*

Dance videos have quickly and subtly become popular with both children and adults alike. However, let me alert you; dance videos are one of Satan's latest weapons in saturating the human mind with pornography. Pay close attention to the content of videos: the way people in the video dress, move, act and appear...they are either partially naked or completely naked. These are all the ingredients of pornography; content designed to produce sexual arousal.

Nevertheless, to further establish the fact of pornography's danger, the United States Congress passed our first anti-pornography law in 1873, according to Brenda Love in *"Encyclopedia of Unusual Sex Practices."* If you follow sexual crimes, the sex offenders in almost all cases, have a history of pornographic involvement. It is at the core of most sex crimes. And most, where not criminalistic, until they started engaging in pornography.

Pornography tempts you to try what you are watching. This is why many, watch a tape, and masturbate, or commit adultery.

Because pornography is a sin, it presents a distorted view of sexuality. Women are presented as objects. Fornication is promoted. Sexual myths and lies are taught. Sex is cheapened, and love is robbed. Pornography exploits the eyes, the mind, and the body.

(ADVICE)

Key Problem: If you are struggling with pornography; this is an issue with the eyes and the mind. It is the captivation of the mind by a sexual presentation made to the eyes.

To overcome pornography, pray, and ask God to help you apply the following steps:

1. Repent- Turn away from this sin and ask God to help you. (*Acts 3:19.*)

2. Avoid visually stimulating material (pornography, dance videos, sexual TV shows etc..) (*1 Thessalonians 5:22.*)

3. Practice refusing ungodly thoughts and images. (*2 Corinthians 10:4,5.*)

4. Avoid ungodly use of the body. (*1 Corinthians 6:20.*)

5. Fill your mind with sexual scriptures. (*Colossians 3:16, 1Corinthians 6:18, 1 Thessalonians 4:3, 2 Timothy 2:22, Colossians 3:5.*)

For additional help and information See *Lust, Nudity, and Fornication.*

Prostitution

Prostitution- is the act of having sex for money. In (*Proverbs 29:3*), the Bible says, "*but a companion of harlots (prostitutes) wastes his wealth.*"

Prostitution is all about your wealth (money.) A person is no more than "money" to a prostitute. Many have referred to the prostitute as a sack chaser. And in essence that is what she does She looks for the opportunity to get her hands on his sack (money.) Her tactic is to lock eyes with her victim.

If you have ever watched a prostitute, whether you are walking, driving, standing or sitting, she will try to establish eye contact. Why? Her seduction is released through the eyes. In (*Proverbs 6:25,*) the scripture says "*Do not lust after her beauty in your heart, nor let her allure you with her eyelids.*" This explains why clients are often referred to as tricks. A prostitute is clever at using her charm and sexuality to trick a man out of his money. This would also explain the origin of the term hooker. A prostitute has mastered the use of sex appeal to both hook a man's mind, and wallet.

However, I want to note that prostitution is not limited to women, but is also practiced by men, who are called gigolos. In (*Deuteronomy 23:18,*) the Bible says "*You shall not bring the wages of a harlot or the price of a dog to the house of the Lord your God for any vowed offering.*" The term "dog" in the Hebrew is "*Keleb*" pronounced (Keh-leb), which means male prostitute.

Even men as early as Bible days engaged in sex for money. However, for the sake of clarity, due to traditional thinking, I will focus on the female aspect of prostitution.

Prostitution has become very modern. The manner in which sex is sold, has become quite diverse. When most people think about prostitution, they think about people who walk the streets of a community to sell sex. But, times have drastically changed. For example, prostitution is presented as an:

Escort service, where a man can request a woman, matching the exact specifications of his fantasy and then have her hand delivered to his house if the price is right.

Massage Parlors provide opportunities to buy sex under the guise of an innocent massage.

Strippers will seduce you through dancing, and once the man is uncontrollably excited, tell him that with a little more money, this can be taken to another level (sex.)

Phone sex gives the deception that selling sex over the phone couldn't hurt a flea.

Mistress is a prostitute, who is in a relationship with her client. The only thing holding that relationship together is sex and money.

Porn stars make films having sex for one reason, money. And did you know that the Greek word used in (*Matthew 21:31,32*), for "harlot" is "porne*" (por-nay.)* Since pornography comes from the same Greek word; this simply says that pornography is a form of prostitution. All of these sexual preferences equal one thing; sex for sale.

This is how sophisticated prostitution has become. However, (*Proverbs 6:26*) says "*For by means of a harlot a man is reduced to a crust of bread.*" Prostitution puts an economical drain on a community. But, in spite of the parasitic effect prostitution has upon cities, states, countries and the world at large, it is a thriving business. In fact one state Nevada, and countries as Australia, Holland and Germany have legalized prostitution. According to officials in Belgium 80,000 people a day visits prostitutes

Prostitution has been protected by organizations designed to promote the rights of sex workers. One such organization is *"The North American Task Force on Prostitution"* founded in 1979.

Furthermore, there are others who protect prostitution: wealthy business men, unhappy men (single or married), bored housewives, curious teenagers, stressed out professional (police, judges, lawyers, politicians.) One writer, Nikki Craft wrote, *"It takes a village to make a prostitute."* Mick Lasalle in *"Hollywood is hooked on hookers"* wrote, *"the prostitute is a victim of every bad thing men do to women: physical and sexual abuse, economic oppression and abandonment."* Every costumer, every belittling comment, every judgmental mind, every negative experience, adds to the making of a prostitute.

Linda Fairstein in *"Sexual Violence: our war against rape"* quotes, *"Whore-subhuman, no rights, invisible and wicked."* This is a quote that reflects the mind set of the world towards prostitutes. However, this is not what God thinks of prostitutes. God loves the prostitute, but hates the prostitution. In (*Hebrews 11:31*), the Bible says, *"By faith the harlot Rahab did not perish with those who did not believe"*; God protected the harlot from being killed.

If you are a prostitute or supporter of prostitution, God does not hate you, He hates the actions.

(ADVICE)

Key Problem: If you are struggling with prostitution; this is an issue with abuse, and low self-esteem. You have suffered an abusive past. You have been beaten with words, thoughts, emotions, situations and circumstances that have lowered you to a life you are not proud of.

To overcome prostitution, pray, and ask God to help you apply the following steps:

1. Repent- Turn away from this sin and ask God to forgive you. (*Acts 3:19.*)

2. Join a Bible teaching/living church. Let God nourish your void through spiritual parents (Pastors) who will speak and deposit positive things into your life. (*Hebrews 10:25, 1 Corinthians 4:15.*)

3. Ministry Group- Join a men's/women's fellowship. Let God nourish you through healthy relationships.

4. Word Study- Take a Bible and Strong's Concordance and look up as many references as you can on love and body.

For additional help and information See *Abuse and Fornication.*

Rape

Rape- the act of having sex with someone, without consent. Due to the complexity of rape, I would like to submit an additional definition of rape, provided by "RAINN", which stands for "*Rape, Abuse, Incest, National Network*" I quote: "*rape is forced sexual intercourse, including both psychological and coercion and physical force. Forced sexual intercourse means vaginal, anal, or oral penetration by the offender(s). This category includes incidents where the penetration is a foreign object such as a bottle.*" Although, each state has their own definition of rape, I believe this definition captures the essence of rape.

Rape is a serious matter. It has been categorized by sexologist as violent sex. According to "RAINN", "*every two minutes someone is raped.*" Moreover, "RAINN" states, "*1 out of 6 women are victims of rape.*"

The "*National Crime Victimization Survey*" (NCVS) has documented the following statistics:

* The average age of a rapist is 31 [1997 NCVS]

* The age group at the highest risk of rape is 12-34 years of age [2000 NCVS]

* The age group most likely to be raped is 16-19 years of age [2000 NCVS]

* 43% of rapes occur between 6pm-12am [1997 NCVS]

* 66% of rape victims knew the perpetrator [1997 NCVS]

* 86% of rapist used physical force [2000 NCVS]

* Rapist stand only a 50% chance of being jailed, when reported [1999] * 61% of rapes went unreported [1999 NCVS]

These are mind boggling facts that reveal the barbaric nature of rape. However, rape presents itself under various circumstances:

(A) Gang rape- forced into sex with a group of people. (*Judges 19:1-30.*)

(B) Military rape- forced into sex by a military member within the military community.

(C) Prison rape- forced into sex by a prison inmate.

(D) Date rape- forced into sex while dating. Generally the drugs *"GHB (gammahydroxbutyrate) and "ecstasy"* which are physiologically altering drugs making one physically weak and imbalanced, are used by rapists during dating.

(E) Marital rape- a spouse forcing the other spouse to have sex. Marital rape is a crime in all 50 states of the US.

(F) Statutory rape- an adult having sex with a minor. It is having sex with someone that falls below the statue's (Law) age of consent

Rape can creep into many places of life, but regardless of the type, it's all the same, sex without consent.

In (*2 Samuel 13:10-19*), the scriptures tell of the story, where Tamar was raped by her brother Amnon; verse 14 says *"he would not heed her voice; and being stronger than she , he forced her and lay with her"*; in verse 12, rape is called a *"foolish or disgraceful act"*, in verse 16, rape is referred to as an act of *"evil."* According to the word of God, rape is a dishonoring sin.

However, lets look a little closer at the text, and identify the elements of rape:

(A) Power-the rapist uses power destructively, to overthrow his victim; verse 14 says, *"Amnon being stronger than she, he forced her and lay with her."*

(B) Violence- the rapist angrily forces himself unto his victim, creating violent circumstances; in verse 14 we saw *Amnon* get violent with *Tamar,* by overpowering her.

(C) Loss- a rapist takes sex from his victim, and with this comes the loss of dignity, respect, security and in some cases, virginity.; verse 14 confirms Tamar's loss. History, tells us she was approximately 15 years old, and a virgin.

(D) Pain-the rapist causes physical, mental and emotional affliction, both for the victim and ironically himself; verse 19 says, *"She went away crying bitterly"*, in verse 15 the Bible says, *"Then Amnon hated her exceedingly, so that the hatred with which he hated her was greater than the love with which he loved her."*

Amnon the rapist, went from loving Tamar to hating her with a deep passion. Rape is like a two-edged sword, it cuts in two directions at the same time. A rapist makes victims, but is also a victim of his own actions.

Nevertheless, we just examined the elements they always surround a rape: power, violence, loss, and pain. Such elements are in total contradiction to the God-ordained nature of sex. Sex was meant to be an experience of blessing, not abuse. (Genesis *1:28*)

I remember the true story of a serial rapist-killer who raped and killed prostitutes. And only after being captured did he confess to the police that his mother was a prostitute, and killing prostitutes after he raped them, was his way of releasing anger towards his mother for her prostitute life.

During the act of rape, many rapist are releasing anger due to a past life of abuse. Many were hurt by a female figure (mother, grandmother, aunt, girlfriend or wife.) And rape becomes a type of revenge, and in some cases a form of security. Exerting force and dominance over a female, can make the rapist feel a sense of control, that he may have lost in his past.

However, to overpower the will of another person, or take something that does not belong to you, or deliberately hurt someone is a sin before God.

This is exactly what rape does.

(ADVICE)

Key Problem: If you are struggling with rape; this is an issue with power, anger, and abuse.

To overcome rape, pray, and ask God to help you apply the following steps:

(Rapist):

1. Repent- Turn away from this sin and ask God to forgive you. (*Acts 3:19.*)

2. Counsel- Get professional Christian counsel. (*Proverbs 11:14.*

. Church- Join a Bible teaching/living church. Submit to godly eadership. (*Hebrews 13:7,17.*)

. Forgive- Pardon everyone who hurt you, especially women. *Mark 11:25.*)

. Avoid anger- Practice refusing bitter thoughts and feelings. *Philippians 4:8, Galatians 5:22.*)

Victim):

ips on preventing rape:

1) Try to date in groups

2) Watch flirtatious communication

3) Watch private places (houses, cars, rooms, parking lots)

4) Avoid provocative dressing

5) Avoid excessive touching

6) Avoid late trips (store ,gas station)

7) Park and walk in lighted places

8) Become aware of where rapes have occurred

f attacked by a rapist:

1) Scream

2) Use car keys as a weapon

3) Try talking to your attacker, to throw him off

4) Stay calm. Don't upset the attacker

5) Stay observant.

6) Try to fight, and break free

If you have been raped:

(1) Get to a safe place

(2) Call for help (someone close, for support)

(3) Call the police

(4) Do not change clothes (needed evidence)

(5) Do not wash up (needed evidence)

(6) Get medical attention

(7) Act swiftly to obtain justice (time is not on your side)

Additional Advice:

(1) Counsel- Get professional spiritual counsel. (*Proverbs 11:14.*)

(2) Don't blame yourself- (*Proverbs 23:7, Mark 11:23.*)

(3) Spent lots of time with God (there is healing in His presence.) (*Isaiah 61:1.*)

For additional help and information See *Abuse.*

Sadism

Sadism- the act of applying pain to become sexually aroused. This act of sex is also associated with other forms of painful sex: Masochism is the act of receiving pain to become sexually aroused. Auto-Masochism is the act of one applying pain to one's own body to create sexual arousal. Sado Masochism is the act of two or more people exchanging the roles of Sadism and Masochism during sexual activity. Each of these forms of sexuality carry the common nature of pain.

However, I want to focus on sadism to discuss some of the common elements that are associated with all of these types of sexual expressions.

In (*Leviticus 20:1-5*), the people of God are warned to not worship Molech; a pagan god, who was known for sex involving pain (*Leviticus 18:21.*) Hence, this type of sex was associated with ungodly and demonic activity.

When you understand the types of things that occur during sadism, it doesn't lead you to a logical conclusion. It appears senseless, and one can see that it is clearly demonic. This is the type of sex, that encourages rough, mean and abusive behavior. People are spanked with a hand, a whip, a paddle. People are slapped, punched, cut, tied up, degrading language and filthy words are exchanged. Much of this behavior involves role playing. But in spite of the sexual playfulness, this type of sex has real consequences. The behavior is animalistic. People are treated like second and third class citizens.

I remember, when I used to work for an Agency as a family therapist. I counseled a husband and wife, who were having marital problems with their sex life. The husband was a mild mannered person. The wife was aggressive, and outspoken. In the bedroom, she desperately wanted her husband to rough her up, and get abusive to become sexually aroused. He loved his wife, and struggled with treating his wife in this degrading manner. This resulted in the wife threatening to divorce her husband, if he didn't harden up.

Needless to say, they did not survive the marriage. In creating what therapist refer to as a biological sketch of a client, I learned that the wife came out of an abusive home. Her mother was extremely abusive towards her father. Because this abusive environment was a way of life, abuse became associated with love. This would explain why some relationships are comfortable with abusive behavior. Abuse is seen as an expression of love and care.

In (*Ephesians 6:4*), the scripture says, "*and you fathers, provoke not your children to wrath; but bring them up in the nurture and admonition of the Lord.*" Children rely upon nurture (instructional care.) It is the type of care that teaches a child how to be properly loved. If it is not received from the parents (especially the father, being the provider for the entire home) a child will grow up and substitute the nourishment with other things (sex, drugs, relationships etc..)

When parents provide proper care for their children, this helps eliminate sexual vulnerability.

(ADVICE)

Key Problem: If you are struggling with sadism; this is an issue with abuse, low self-esteem and nurture.

To overcome sadism, pray, and ask God to help you apply the following steps:

1. Repent- Turn away from this sin and ask God to forgive you. (*Acts 3:19.*)

2. Church- Join a Bible teaching/living church. Let God nurture you through spiritual parents (Pastors) who will "speak" and "deposit" positive things into your life. (*Ephesians 4:11,12, 1Corinthians 4:15.*)

3. Ministry Group- Join a men's/women's fellowship. Allow God to nurture you through healthy relationships. (Hebrews 10:25.)

4. Word Study- Take a Bible and a Strong's Concordance and look up as many references as you can on love (God's.)

For additional help and information See *Abuse.*

Sexual Harassment

Sexual Harassment- the act of annoying someone with sexual intentions. Due to the nature of this subject I want to provide an additional definition on sexual harassment. The *"British Columbia Human Rights Commission"* defines sexual harassment as *"unwelcomed conduct of a sexual nature that has a negative effect on where you work, or live, or receive services."*

In (*Genesis 39:4-12*), the Bible records the classic story of sexual harassment. A handsome young man by the name of Joseph, was persistently pursued by his Master's wife with sexual passion. This text reveals the main components of sexual harassment. But, before I elaborate on these characteristics. I want to present a relevant quote from *"Harassment Hotline Inc."* This organization states that there are three general areas to sexual harassment:

(1) Verbal- including epithets (descriptive names or titles) derogatory comments or slurs that are based on sex.

(2) Physical- assault, impending or blocking movement or any physical interference with normal work or movement when directed at an individual based on sex.

(3) Visual- includes derogatory, posters, cartoons or drawings based on sex."

These three elements: verbal, physical, and visual covers the basic make-up of sexual harassment.

However, I believe that these three areas are only expressions of a greater problem; dishonor and respect. Sexual harassment is about overstepping boundaries. When the line of human rights are drawn, and a person disregards it, it is a clear message of no respect. No respect, regards or consideration for your rights as a human being.

Thus, sexual harassment is a respect issue.

However, lets return to the text and discuss the three areas in which disrespect has become pervasive.

First, King Potiphar's wife disrespected Joseph with "words" (*Ephesians 4:29.*) She spoke to Joseph inappropriately; verse 7 records her saying, "*lie with me.*"

Second, Potiphar's wife disrespected Joseph with her "body" (*Romans 12:1.*) She blocked Joseph, and threw her self upon him; verse 12 says, "*she caught him by his garment.*"

Third, Potiphar's wife disrespected Joseph with her "eyes" (*Job 31:1.*) She stared at him, with eyes of lust, verse 7 says, "*She cast long (staring) eyes on Joseph.*"

The story of Joseph and King Potiphar's wife, teach us that sexual harassment is about disrespect with either words, the body or the eyes.

And in the sight of God is an intolerable sin. (Genesis *39:9.*)

(ADVICE)

Key Problem: If you are struggling with sexual harassment; this is an issue with respect or honor.

To overcome sexual harassment, pray, and ask God to help you apply the following steps:

(Harasser):

If you are a sexual harasser, the Bible says, in (*1 Corinthians 12:10,*) "*Be kindly affectionate to one another with brotherly love in [honor] giving preference to one another.*" The word honor in this passage means to esteem, value, or "*respect.*"

1. Repent- Turn away from this sin and ask God to forgive you. (*Acts 3:19.*)

2. Practice honoring people (friends, neighbors, church members family members, strangers.) (*1 Corinthians 12:10.*)

3. Word Study- Take a Bible and the Strong's Concordance and look up as many references as you can on honor.

4. Counsel- Get professional Christian counsel. (*Proverbs 11:14.*)

(Victim):

Here are some things to do, according to "The British Columbia Human Rights Commission":

1. Keep Records- times, dates, witnesses.

2. Talk about it- share the incident with others, to create support

3. Let the harasser know what you think

4. Report the harassment

5. Get help from the community (legal advice, support groups, churches)

God can heal you and restore your self-confidence and dignity (*Isaiah 61:1.*)

And remember, no one deserves to be disrespected in any form of the word, especially sexually.

Sexual Worship

Sexual Worship- the act of using sexual activity as a means of entering spiritual worship. In (*Deuteronomy 23:17,18,*) the scriptures teach on the law that prohibits temple prostitution. The nation of Israel was told not to conduct prostitution in the temple, and not to take the money earned from prostitution and offer it as a vow to God. This was a hypocritical and sacrilegious act of combining sex and worship.

The temple prostitute had sex with the intention of worshipping

God with her earnings. In some churches, women are convinced that they are offering service to God by satisfying their Pastor in a sexual manner.

It is a temple prostitute mentality. In (*Proverbs 7:14,15*), the scripture says, "*I have peace offerings with me; today I have paid my vows. So I came out to meet you, diligently to seek your face, and I have found you.*" The text is about a woman who boasts of her religious devotion. "*Peace offerings and vows*" were apart of the Mosaic law, and spoke of her so called commitment to religion. After worshipping God, she celebrates her worship with sexual immorality. It is a clear case of joining sex and worship.

However, there is a growing form of sexuality called Tantra sex. According to "*Tantra. Com*", tantra comes from tan which means to extend, continue or prolong. This type of sex is based in India, and is defined as the act of learning how to delay sexual orgasms through meditation and yoga techniques to achieve spiritual completeness. The philosophy of tantra, believes that one can use sex to enter a realm of spiritual worship and wholeness. Moreover, tantra sex incorporates the teachings of Hinduism and Buddhism making it paganistic and cultic in nature. (Exodus *20:3.*)

This brings us to another distorted approach towards sex, where sex is used therapeutically, which they are called sex surrogates. According to "*Psychology Today*" June 2003; sex surrogates are "*part of a team working with mental health practitioners to help clients overcome intimacy obstacles. Surrogates use exercises in communication, relaxation and social-skills training, as well as sensual and sexual touching. Intercourse occurs only when [clinically necessary].*" This is another attempt to use sex to do only what God and the word of the Lord can do.

However, the most common form of sexual worship is the idolization of sex itself. Many believe that sex answers everything

If you're lonely have sex. If you're angry have sex. If you need peace of mind, have sex. If you need to verify your soul-mate have sex with them. Sex becomes the crutch that many will lean upon as a twisted form of support, to fulfill service unto God. How many people have said "*I need a man or woman to stay in church*." How many people are inconsistent in their relationship with God, when there are "sexual problems" with their lovers.

When this occurs, we have connected "God and sex." You cannot connect worshipping God to sex. God is God, all by Himself; He doesn't need our sexuality as a channel into His deity. (*Genesis 17:1.*)

Sexual worship is a subtle attempt by Satan to pervert *"true worship"* and deceive the true worshippers. Remember, according to (*Genesis 1:28*), God gave sex to man. Man cannot give sex to God. Sexual worship is an act that comes out of sexual intention, but spiritual worship is an act that comes out of *"heart conviction."* There must be a change of motive; seeking God with the heart, not an experience.

(ADVICE)

Key Problem: If you are struggling with sexual worship; this is an issue with idolatry. It is one seeking to use sex to fulfill spiritual wholeness, which only God can do.

To overcome sexual worship, pray, and ask God to help you apply the following steps:

1. Repent- Turn away from this sin and ask God to forgive you. (*Acts 3:19.*)

2. Avoid ungodly sex. (*1 Thessalonians 4:3.*)

3. Learn to worship God on "truth" (the Bible.) (*St. John 14:6.*)

4. Avoid any religious practice that does not place Jesus Christ at the center. (*3 John 1:7-9.*)

5. Word Study- Take a Bible and a Strong's Concordance and look up as many references as you can on worship and idol.

Shacking

Shacking- the act of a man and woman living together outside of marriage. In (*1 Timothy 4:1-3*), the scriptures says, Now the Spirit expressly says that in latter times some will depart from the faith, giving heed to deceiving spirits and doctrines of demons. Speaking lies in hypocrisy, having their own conscience seared with a hot iron. Forbidding to marry. Notice verse 3 *Forbidding to marry*; Shacking is a detour from marriage. It is saying I want the benefits of marriage, but not marriage. In verse 1, the scripture says "*giving heed to deceiving spirits and doctrines of demons.*" Did you know that forbidding to marry (shacking) is a doctrine or teaching from demon spirits? In other words anybody who believes in living together before marriage is being deceived and indoctrinated by the Devil.

Moreover in (*Genesis 2:15-25*), the Bible gives the correct example of cohabitation; in verse 15, we see God placing the man (Adam) into the Garden. And the Garden of Eden becomes the dwelling place for the only man on earth; in verse 18, God says, "*It is not good for man to be alone*", which indicated the social nature of man; so in verses 21,22, God puts Adam to sleep, and creates Eve out of the man. Incredible. And in verse 22, "*God*" brings Eve to the man (Adam).

Now, remember where Adam is (the Garden of Eden.) Now, God has both Adam and Eve living in the Garden, and guess what he calls them? Verse 25 says "*And they were both naked, the man and his wife were not ashamed.*" If God called Eve, Adam's wife, Adam had to be her husband. My point is simple; the only two people that God will allow to live together in the setting of romance, is husband and wife.

Shacking goes against God's original plan for co-habitation. Moreover, the Bible presents another example of shacking in (*St. John 4:18*), the amplified translation reads "*For you have had five husbands and the man you are now living with is not your husband.*" A clear case of shacking. Notice she had five husbands, and the man she was shacking with, was not her husband. Shacking does not equip you for marriage, it keeps you from marriage.

People are not encouraged to marry, if they are already getting the benefits of marriage. Which reminds me of the old cliche regarding milk, which says, why go after the bottle, when I already have the cow. If you allow a man to live married, it does not make a lot of sense to get married. Most marriage experts agree that the majority of people who live together before marriage, end up divorcing. When two people decide to live together before marriage they are robbed of control. Two people who wait, develop control power. The ability to control potentially threatening behavior. This is unquestionably necessary for a healthy marriage.

Moreover, I have counseled multitudes of people, and in most of the cases of shacking, the couples never got married. However, some of the reasons for living together outside of the marriage has been anything from hilarious to unbelievable. But, there are some which I believe stands out: Many will say, "we're testing the waters." Many believe experience is the best teacher. Listen, you don't need to experience cancer to understand that cancer is deadly.

The Holy Spirit is called the Teacher in (*St. John 14:26*), and He will teach you everything you need to know about another person. Moreover, in (*Genesis 3:22*), God brought Eve to Adam. God is the best match maker in the world. God knows how to bring you the right person. Many will live together for convenience. You might hear, "I got put out, and I have no where to live, can I come live with you." Or "You live over there, and I live over here, why don't we come together and save money." Or "we have a child together, and we need to move in with one another to see if things can work." Did any of these sound familiar?

Nevertheless, shacking presents real dangers to the institution of the family life. As I said earlier shacking does not prepare the way for marriage, it destroys it. Moreover, it leads to pregnancy, which most couples are not prepared for. Now, you have a child born out of wedlock. And did you know, that the judgment of God comes with this experience (*Hebrews 13:4.*) And I don't want to be misunderstood; God is not against the baby; He is against sex outside of marriage. This is why couples who move together and have children outside of marriage, never seem to find peace.

There is definitely a divine judgment on the relationship. In most cases the couple eventually break up, and now you have a split-family, and two part-time parents raising a full-time baby. It's a mess.

Co-habitation is a marital benefit. It is the long awaited prize. It is the opportunity to completely join lives. Yet, if entered into too soon, is like plucking the apple before it ripens, its bitter every time.

(ADVICE)

Key Problem: If you are struggling with shacking; this is an issue with marriage. It is failing to understand the value and sacredness of the marriage covenant.

To overcome shacking, pray, and ask God to help you apply the following steps:

1. Repent- Turn away from this sin and ask God to forgive you (*Acts 3:19.*)

2. Move out- Stop living with your lover. (*Hebrews 12:1.*)

3. Virginity- Start over with God, and begin living "like" a virgin. Abstain from sex. (*1 Thessalonians 4:3.*)

4. Counsel- If you are serious about your lover, seek marital counsel. (*Proverbs 11:14.*)

5. Word Study- Take a Bible and a Strong's Concordance and look up as many references as you can on marriage.

Sexually Transmitted Diseases

Sexually Transmitted Diseases (STDS)- a disease that is contracted or obtained by sexual activity. Sexually transmitted diseases(STDS) are one of the all too common and horrible consequences of sexual sin. According to *"Unspeakable; The Naked truth about STDS"*, "One out of five people are infected with a STD. To clarify the magnitude of this fact, *ASHA (American Social Health Association)* says, that it cost about 8 billion dollars a year to treat STDS. This amount of money indicates the extreme numbers of infected people.

Above all, this information confirms the alarming nature of sexual immorality. In (*1Corinthians 6:18*), the scripture says, *"But he who commits sexual immorality sins against his own body."* In (*Proverbs 6:33*), the scriptures say, wounds and dishonor he will get, and his reproach will not be wiped away." The word wound in the Hebrew is nega pronounced (neh-gah) which means figuratively a blow, and literally a spot or disease; in verses 20-35 of this chapter, the writer is speaking of sexual immorality and it's consequences, which this passage tells us that sexual sin can and does result in diseases and injury to the body. Moreover, in (*Hebrews 13:4*), the scriptures declare *"Marriage is honorable among all, and the bed undefiled; but fornicators and adulterers*

God will judge". Sexually transmitted diseases are without question a judgment of God. These detestable conditions are the result of violating the sexual laws of God. Nevertheless, there are more than 30 types of STDS, but I would like to identify the most common infections, taken from *"Safe Sex"* by *Joe S. McIlhaney Jr. M.D.*:

(A) Chlamydia- an infection caused by a microorganism that causes damage to the uterus, tubes and ovaries of a woman, and discharge of the penis in a man.

(B) HPV Human Papillomavirus)- an infection caused by a virus that produces genital warts.

(C) Gonorrhea (Claps)- an infection that is caused by a bacterium (*gonococcus*) that results in the discharge of pus from the vagina or penis.

(D) Hepatitis B- is an infection caused by a virus that affects the functioning of the liver.

(E) Herpes- is an infection caused by a virus that produces blisters and sores in and on the sex organ.

(F) Syphilis- is an infection caused by a bacterium (spirochete) that can result in total bodily damage, especially of the brain, heart and nerves.

(G) Trichomoniasis (Vaginitis)- is an infection caused by a parasite that produces burning and itching in the vaginal area, and discharge from the penis.

(H) AIDS (Acquired Immune Deficiency Syndrome) is the condition of a destroyed immune system caused by the HIV virus Due to the more serious nature of this disease, I want to provide additional data. The following information is based upon *"The Time Almanac, 2003."* According to history, AIDS was discovered in sub-Saharan, Africa in the year 1985. To date, 40 million people in the world is documented as living with AIDS; 28.5 million is documented having died from AIDS. The means of contracting AIDS can happen in three primary ways:

(a) sex with an infected person,

(b) sharing a hypodermic needle, or pricked by a needle that was shared with an infected person,

(c) Breast feeding. To date, there is no known cure for AIDS, but medication that will retard or slow down the effects of the virus has been invented.

Moreover, the following are general symptoms for sexually transmitted diseases:

* Discharge of pus from the genitals

* Burning during urination

* Genital growths

* Genital Sores

* Skin rashes or sores

* Enlarged lymph nodes

* Long lasting infections

* Yellow eyes-dark urine

* Itching of the pubic hair

However, according to medical experts 80% of the STD cases have no symptoms. The main route of STDS into the body is bodily fluids (blood, blood derived products, semen, vaginal fluids and saliva.) It is also important to note that STDS can enter the body through cracks or cuts in the skin.

Amazingly, for such life threatening infections, STDS are very weak outside of their environment: warmth and moisture. STDS quickly die without warmth and moisture, including the HIV virus. This dispels the myth of catching a disease through a handshake, hugging or any other non-fluid contact. But, also explains why women are prone to more damage caused by an STD then men. Because of the design of the women's genitalia, she has more area for moisture, and thus, is more susceptible to such diseases.

Which brings us to another vulnerable population, teens. Some doctors believe that it is a fact that teens are at greater risk in contracting STDS. Because, unlike adults who have had more exposure to germs, causing the body to develop the ability to fight off more germs, resulting in health conditions that germs cannot survive within, teens may not have the same fight power due to less exposure. Also teens are at greater risk because, they take more sexual risk.

Leading experts agree that the following are the most common reasons for the rapid spreads of STDS:

1. New Strains- new diseases are developing that do not respond to antibiotics or medical treatment.

2. Non use of contraceptives- many do not wear protection.

3. High Mobility- infected people are having more sex with more partners.

4. No Education- most people are not informed about how to prevent infection and/or what to do if infected.

5. Lack of treatment- many people go untreated.

6. Symptomless Carriers- many are infected and don't know it.

7. Lack of reporting by medical doctors- many doctors do not report the STDS cases, causing statistics to be much lower and incapable of presenting the true level of danger.

Condoms also play an important role in the transmission of STDS. The reason for this misfortune is that many believe condoms are 100 % safe. Many have failed to understand that condoms break and are used improperly. And some people say, condoms are very safe due to the extensive testing before packaging. Not true. Listen to the following information; Joe S. McIlhaney Jr. M.D. in *"Safe Sex"* states, *"The FDA allows condom manufacturers to market condoms that have three or fewer holes per 1000 condoms. Condoms rupture about 7 percent of the time during use."* Now, based upon these facts; a condom doesn't sound so safe. This says the next condom that you use, like Russian Roulette, could be the bullet in the chamber or the defected condom.

Surely, your life is worth more than putting such blind trust in the hands of an imperfect manufacturer, who has an imperfect success rate of producing imperfect condoms. Remember, condoms provide very little safety for the body and absolutely no safety for the heart.

Moreover, some believe that once you contract a STD. You build up immunity against re-infection. This is simply not true because medical experts have declared that the body cannot produce antibodies against these type (STDS) of diseases. This would explain why thousands are re-infected.

Sexually Transmitted Diseases are not the will of God. They are the result of sin. In (*Exodus 15:22-26*), the Bible teaches, that if the Nation of Israel sinned against God, sicknesses would have been the end result.

In (*Matthew 24:3-7*), the Bible speaks of the word "pestilences" as worldwide conditions that will serve as a sign of the end times. In other words the epidemical spread of STDS are one of the signs that the world is coming to an end; Jesus is coming soon.

(ADVICE)

Key Problem: If you are struggling with STDS; this is an issue with safety.

However, true safety is not about "safe sex" but rather "pure sex." In (*1 Thessalonians 4:3*), the scripture says, "F*or this is the will of God , your sanctification: that you should abstain from sexual immorality.*" This passage reveals the solution to STDS; Abstinence. It's about pure sex not safe sex. In light of the facts presented in this discussion, safe sex is not so safe.

To overcome STDS, pray, and ask God to help you apply the following steps:

1. Sexual Education- Learn what God has to say about sex. Study secular information on sexuality under the guidance of the word. (Proverbs 7:1-5.)

2. Avoid sex before marriage. (*1 Thessalonians 4:3.*)

3. Avoid sex outside of marriage. (*Hebrews 13:5.*)

4. Understand that "marriage" is the only realm where sex is "blessed" and thus, safe. (*Genesis 1:28.*)

For additional help and information See *Fornication.*

Soul-ties

Soul-ties- the act of being emotionally, mentally and willfully joined to a person or an act through sexual activity. If you are in sexua danger, and in spite of efforts to break free, you find yourself going through a revolving door of sexual games and chaos, you are facing a soul-tie. Many have addictive behavior towards people, or things or situations, and this addiction has nothing to due with drugs. It is uncontrollable behavior that evolves around sexual immorality. It is something that I know is wrong, but I can't seem to break free of it. It is the tying of your mind, emotions and will. It is a soul-tie.

Lets look at the meaning of the soul, more closely. Every person has a soul (*Genesis 2:7, 1 Thessalonians 5:23.*) The make up of the soul is threefold: the mind, the emotions, and the will. A soul-tie involves the tying or uniting of each one of these areas (mind, emotions, will) with the person or activity that sex was committed with, which brings us to the origin of soul-ties.

How is a soul-tie created? In (*1 Corinthians 6:16*), the Bible says, *"or do you not know that he who is joined to a harlot is one body with her? For the two He says, shall become one flesh."* These words help us understand the power of sex. This scripture teaches us that when sexual activity occurs there is a joining effect between the parties that are involved.

In other words sex has joining, uniting or tying power. A soul-tie is simply created by engaging in sexual activity. This is why one night stands should be called lifetime stands, because what happens in a night of sexual fun create effects that can last throughout a life time. For example, a woman can meet a man, have sex with him on the first date, and later find out that he has several girlfriends, and end up feeling betrayed. Why would she portray that type of attachment in such a short period of time? Because, the body is a medium through which the soul can be touched. A one night stand appears to be over in one night, but in reality it's not the ending, it's the beginning of another "touch." A man can touch a woman's soul by touching her body.

This is how two people can bond and get so close to one another even after having just met.

Sex has joining power, and each experience is a touch of the soul. And the souls of many have been covered in many finger prints, where each finger print bears the personality of the sexual partner.

This is why a promiscuous person can take on a lot of strange ways that cannot be explained. All of these partners are inside of the person in the sense of their "perpetual influence."

Furthermore, because sex leads to such drastic changes in a person's behavior, it confirms that sex leaves a deposit. I am reminded of a story that was told to a renown minister; *Pastor Creflo Dollar of World Changers Ministries International*, by his father. The story was entitled *"A stick in a hole."* His father made a line of three holes in the ground; he grabbed a nearby stick and proceeded to place the stick in the first hole. When he proceeded to take the stick out of the first hole, and place it into the second hole, the stick accumulated dirt from the first hole, and the process repeated with the third hole. Nevertheless, the moral of the story was, Keep your stick out of other people's holes.

Pastor Dollar's father wanted his son to ultimately understand that every time you have sex with someone two things happen: you receive a deposit, and you make a deposit. You literally, sleep with everybody who slept with the person you had sex with. These deposits continue to accumulate into a breakdown of healthy thinking, healthy decisions, and healthy feelings; where a person experiences that destructive cycle of satisfaction; the soul-tie. It's the experience of desiring something that I know is destroying me but yet, I want it. Which, the Bible refers to as a judgment against the soul (*Proverbs 6:32.*)

Returning to the passage of the scripture in (*1 Corinthians 6:16*) the scripture says, "*He who is joined to a harlot*" it is important to note that in (*Hosea 4:12*), the Bible teaches that harlotry carries the "*spirit of whoredom*" that is, sexual demons are involved in the activity of prostitution (or any form of ungodly sex.) What this means, is when a person commits sexual immorality, they are not only joined to another person, but also to the sexual demons that are present in that individual. This is a deposit by a transference of spirits. In other words, you can pick up demon spirits by having sex.

Nevertheless, the soul-tie works off of the principle of "*sowing and reaping.*" In (*Galatians 6:7*), the scripture says, "*whatever a man sows, he shall also reap.*" Every act of sex is a seed or form of sowing. It is an act of planting. Every time a person commits sexual immorality, this seed produces a harvest or the ability to do the same thing. Whatever you sow is what you get back.

Moreover, the first time a person commits sexual immorality their soul is joined to the soul of the sex partner. However, the more the two partners have sex with one another the stronger the union becomes, making the soul-tie deadlier with each experience. Furthermore, this is the same way an iniquity is developed. The term means to bend. It is something done so many times that one is likely to lean or turn in that direction. It is where you are most tempted to display habits. But thank God, the Bible teaches, in (*Isaiah 53:5*), that Jesus was "*bruised for our iniquities.*"

Good news, Jesus can destroy habits. Nevertheless, because sex is like a seed, there is another law or principle to consider. (*Genesis 1:12*), says, "*The herb that yields seed according to it's kind.*" What this means is that even the type of sex you have will determine the type of soul-tie that is experienced. For example, a pornographer may not be tempted by incest or homosexuality, and vise versa a homosexual may not be turned on by pornography. But a pornographer will be strongly tempted by pornography, because here is where his or her soul is tied.

(ADVICE)

Key Problem: If you are struggling with soul-ties; this is an issue with addiction, low-self esteem and nurture. You are going through motions of *"uncontrollable behavior."* Most soul-ties originate in a hunger to satisfy a childhood void. In (*Ephesians 6:4*) the scripture say, *"And ye fathers provoke not your children to wrath, but bring them up in the nurture and admonition of the Lord"*. God expects parents to provide total nurturing for their children. The reason for this is that children need plenty of nourishing. If children miss this tender season of nurturing, they will seek it in other things (relationships, drugs, alcohol, sex, work.) A person who keeps going back or continues to hold on is looking for nourishment.

A soul-tie is an unhealthy *"union."* Unions are destroyed by unions. In (*1 Corinthians 6:17*), the Bible says, *"But he that is joined unto the Lord is one spirit"*. In the preceding verse (v16), the Bible speaks of the union with a harlot, but verse 17 speaks of the union with the Lord. In other words the only way to destroy a union or soul-tie is to join your soul to God. In (*Galatians 5:16*), the Bible says, *"I say then walk in the Spirit, and you shall not fulfill the lust of the flesh."* The word in speaks to the union that God desires to have with our lives. The union is experienced as we totally surrender to the word of God. (*St. John 6:63*), says *"the words that I speak unto you, they are spirit, and they are life."* The word of God is spirit or spiritual. Thus, we walk in spiritual union with God, by applying the word of God to our life And this consistent fellowship with the Spirit of God will create a union that no soul-tie will ever break.

To overcome soul-ties, pray, and ask God to help you apply the following steps:

1. Repent- Turn away from this sin and ask God to forgive you. (*Acts 3:19.*)

2. Church- Join a Bible teaching/living church. Allow God to nourish you through spiritual parents (Pastors) who will "speak" and "deposit" positive things into your life. (*1 Corinthians 4:15.*)

3. Ministry Group- Join a men's/women's fellowship. Allow God to nourish you through healthy relationships. (*Hebrews 10:25.*)

4. Please see steps to a spiritual schedule under [*Addiction*].

Stalking

Stalking- the act of persistently and dangerously pursuing someone for sexual pleasure. For additional defining, according to "*Angels in Blue*"; stalking is "*a willful course of conduct involving repeated or continuing harassment of another individual that would cause a reasonable person to feel terrorized, frightened, intimidated, threatened, harassed or molested and that actually causes the victim to feel terrorized, frightened, intimidated, threatened, harassed or molested.*"

According to "*Survivors of Stalking Inc.*" *(SOS)*, "*1,006,970 women and 370,992 men are stalked each year in the U.S., and 80% of these targets are women.*"

Stalking has quickly gained national attention, becoming illegal in all 50 states. According to S.O.S. (Survivors *of Stalking*), "*Most violent crimes begin with stalking.*" Stalking creates a "*hunter-hunted*" circumstance.

Stalkers can come in different sizes, appearance, and backgrounds. However, in spite of differences, inside the mind of every stalker is a hunter.

The person is in reckless pursuit of another individual, placing the person being pursued at serious risk. Yet, it is also interesting to note, that a stalker's intentions are not always destructive. Sometimes a stalking episode, although dangerous, because of the fear and emotional injury that can be caused for the victim is more or less a matter of uncontrolled zeal.

The stalker may not have meant any harm, but perhaps came on too strong, and did not know how to let go. Nevertheless, to not make light, it is this component that provokes the stalker, escape. In most cases the stalker is exposed, after a bitter breakup with a significant other or a flirtatious approach that didn't go over well resulting in that infamous one word response, no.

A break-up or rejection can be interpreted by the stalker as an attempt to escape or run, and at this point the chase is on.

Uncontrolled passion can change a harmless person into a relentless monster.

In (*Genesis 39:1-13*), the Bible records the story of a stalking experience. It is the story of Joseph; a young handsome man who loved God, and was sexually pursued by the wife of an Egyptian officer (*Potiphar.*) She stalked Joseph day by day, but he escaped. Joseph escaped the stalker, because he said no. Saying no, was taking a stand to not buy into the game of stalker.

(ADVICE)

Key Problem: If you are struggling with stalking; this is an issue with abuse, nurture, low self-esteem and fear.

To overcome stalking, pray, and ask God to help you apply the following steps:

(Stalker):

1. Repent- Turn away from this sin and ask God to forgive you. (Acts 3:19.)

2. Counsel- Get professional Christian counsel. (*Proverbs 24:6.*)

3. Church- Join a Bible teaching/living church. Allow God to nourish you through spiritual parents (Pastors) who will speak and deposit positives things onto your life. (*Hebrews 10:25, 1 Corinthians 4:15.*)

4. Ministry Groups- Join a men's/women's fellowship and allow God to teach you how to build healthy relationships. (*Acts 2:40-46.*)

5. Word Study- Take a Bible and a Strong's Concordance and look up as many references on love, anger, and fear.

(Victim):

1. Take firm action- Refuse any advances and "never" play with a stalker. (*Genesis 39:1-13.*)

2. Take your time- Don't move quick, when you are just meeting someone. You don't really know who you're dealing with.

God expects couples to get to know each other. And that the true fruit or actions of an individual can only be known over a period of time. (*1 Timothy 5:24, Matthew 7:20, Deuteronomy 24:5, 1 Peter 3:7.*)

3. Do not mislead- Watch your words, your attire, and how you present yourself. Don't do anything that would provoke the stalker. Keep your motives pure. (*Matthew 5:8, Ephesians 4:25.*)

4. Separate peacefully- If you break up with someone, the break up is hard enough; the way you separate can have lasting consequences. You can avoid a lot of potential danger by ending a relationship or association in a peaceful and respectful manner. (*Hebrews 12:14.*)

5. Contact your local police- If you are pursued by a stranger or someone who will not respect your decision to end the acquaintance, involve the authorities.

For additional help and information See *Abuse*.

Sugar Daddy

Sugar Daddy- an older man who is sexually aroused by a younger woman by providing for her as a father figure. The relationship between a sugar daddy and a young woman is based on business. He has a fixed purpose, and she has a fixed purpose. He has a need to nurture or provide for her. She has a need to be mentored, taught and fathered. Both the sugar daddy and the younger woman have a clear understanding that the relationship is more of a business proposition. You take care of me, and I'll take care of you.

It is from this premise that the sugar daddy developed his name. It is an older man who is driven by a need to act like a daddy figure, by providing the sugar (clothes, cars, rent, nails and hair done, allowance, trips, etc.) for a younger woman. Thus, you have a sugar daddy.

For some it's not as complicated, but more like a one night stand. I've known older guys to take advantage of a younger woman who happened to be hungry. He offers to buy her a happy meal from a fast food restaurant, and she agrees to go back to his house to watch a couple of videos, and folks, we know what happens next (sex in exchange for a meal.)

It's a sugar daddy experience on a small scale. Women, don' become somebody's happy meal.

Sociologists refer to this type of sexuality as *"cross-generationa sex.*" It is two people from two different generations, uniting their age groups through a sexual relationship. The question may arise, is it wrong for an older man to date or marry a younger woman? I believe age does not necessarily make or break a relationship. People of substantial age difference enter relationships with one another all the time.

Some of these relationships fail, and some succeed. To answer the question, I don't believe that it is morally wrong for an older man to enter a relationship with a younger woman. The sugar daddy is not a matter of age, but a matter of need. Self-centered needs.

The motive of the sugar daddy changes the entire relationship. It becomes wrong when two people enter an intimate relationship without the foundation of "love" (Ephesians *5:28.*)

However, the sugar daddy relationships are short lived, lasting on an average of one year or less. But, this is not surprising due to the fact that the relationship is held together by weak thread. This weakness is evident in the background of both parties: a history of cheating, a fear of the woman leaving the sugar daddy for a younger man, or a fear of the man going back to his wife, and the younger women suddenly left without income, or both people having a mind-set that this is a game of cat and mouse at best. The relationship is based on sugar and sugar runs out.

In (*Genesis 2:24*), the scripture says "*Therefore a man shall leave his father and mother and be joined to his wife, and they shall become one flesh.*"

Notice the plan of God for a man and woman, in preparation for marriage;

God calls the man and woman away from the priority of the parent-child relationship. Which says, when two people enter a marriage, God does not intend for the parent-child mentality to come with the marriage. God calls a man away from his father, not to act like a daddy towards his wife, but to act like husband.

Simply put, God did not intend for the couple to act like a parent and a child. Remember, the sugar daddy acts like a father, which places the woman in the role of a child. Moreover, (*Ephesians 6:1*), speaks of parents and connects them with children; verse 4; mentions the term fathers and connects the term to "*children.*" In scripture the term father is never connected to the words "*lover or wife.*" The sugar daddy figure goes against the God ordained roles for a man and woman. God expects a couple to relate to each other as man and woman, not father and daughter.

If you are in this type of relationship, end it. It's not secure, and is an accident looking to happen.

(ADVICE)

Key Problem: If you are struggling with the life of a sugar daddy; this is an issue with nurture. If you are the woman, you are looking for a missing part of your childhood. In (*Ephesians 6:4*), notice the word "nurture." It means to "*instruct with care.*" It is the responsibility of the father to nourish the children. But, If a child does not get this nourishment, they will seek it in other things (drugs, sex, relationships, etc.) If you are the man in this relationship, you also seek the same nourishment that was not properly imparted at childhood. More than likely, you may have lost your father or was abandoned by your father as a child. And might have had siblings, who you were forced to help raise like a father figure, or as a child was placed in similar circumstances, where you were forced to grow up before your time.

Whether you are a man or a woman, allow God to Father you (*2 Corinthians 6:17,18.*)

To overcome the life of a sugar daddy, pray and ask God to help you apply the following steps:

1. Repent- Turn away from this sin and ask God to forgive you. (Acts 3:19.)

2. Check your motive in dating people outside your age group.

3. Church - Join a Bible teaching/living church. Allow God to nourish you through spiritual parents (Pastors.) (*1 Corinthians 4:15.*)

4. Ministry Groups- Join a men's/women's fellowship. Allow God to help you build healthy relationships. (Hebrews 10:25.)

5. Word Study- Take a Bible and the Strong's Concordance and look up as many references as you can on love (God's.)

Tattoos

Tattoos- the act of marking the body for sexual purposes. For the sake of clarification, I do not believe that a tattoo in itself is unscriptural.

However, there is a growing popularity with the misuse of tattoos. Tattoos are being placed on private parts of the body, and exposed through scantly dressing, or outright nakedness. When the marking of a tattoo is worn for sexually-immoral purposes, it is a promotion of sexual corruption.

In (*Leviticus 19:28*), the scripture says, "*you shall not make any cuttings in your flesh for the dead, nor tattoo any marks on you: I am the Lord*". In the text the Hebrew word for "tattoo" is "*nathan*" pronounced (naw-than); it means to print or make a mark. It was a sin before God, for the nation of Israel to misuse their bodies with improper markings. However, a tattoo is a presentation of the body. The Bible says in (*Romans 12:1*), says, "*I beseech you therefore brethren by the mercies of God, that you present your bodies a living sacrifice, holy, acceptable to God, which is your reasonable service."* God literally wants your body presented to him.

Moreover, the scripture says, in (*Colossians 3:17*), "*And whatever you do in word or deed do all in the name of Jesus Christ.*" God expects man to make everything he does a reflection of God. Hence, whatever you do with your body should promote a "*godly image.*"

Speaking of images, tattoos are presentations of images. (Exodus 20:4), says, "*you shall not make yourself any carved image or any likeness of anything that is in the earth beneath, or that is in the water under the earth.*" God prohibited the nation of Israel from unhealthy practices with images. If tattoos that do not promote God, is a challenge for you, understand the struggle is in two areas:

(1) proper presentation of the body

(2) watching what and who I am representing

And if you have permanent tattoos that you are not proud of, today's technology provides the opportunity to have them removed. In (*Acts 19:19,*) witches who became Christians, burned their witchcraft books. Some things are well in order to have removed after having removed ourselves from the lifestyle that was associated with it. Allow God to do a new thing, and let your body tell the world, I represent God.

(ADVICE)

Key Problem: If you are struggling with tattoos, this is an issue with representation and presentation.

To overcome tattoos, pray, and ask God to help you apply the following steps:

1. Repent- Turn away from this sin and ask God to forgive you. (*Acts 3:19.*)

2. Focus on wearing things that represent your commitment to God. (*1 Timothy 2:9*)

3. Understand that your main purpose in life is to please God. (*Revelation 4:11.*)

4. Word Study- Take a Bible and the Strong's Concordance and look up as many references a you can on image (God) and body.

Transsexual

Transsexual- the act of seeking to change from one sex gender to another. This expression of sexuality is complex in nature. The person desiring what medical doctors call gender reassignment feels the uncomfortable condition of being trapped inside of the wrong body.

I believe the real struggle with a transsexual lies within the issue of identity. I believe that there is an identity conflict within the mind of the transsexual. The premise for this conflict can be found in (*Romans 1:25.*) which says, "*who exchanged the truth of God for the lie, and worshipped and served the creature rather than the Creator, who is blessed forever Amen.*" Lets focus on the words "*who exchanged the truth of God for the lie.*"

God is saying, when you do not accept the truth of God's word, you open your life to the lies of Satan. In (*St. John 8:44*), the Bible says "*Satan is the father of lies.*" The word father means source, which says, when ever you are lied to about who you are, Satan is behind it. It is the very nature of the Devil to deceive or lead you away from the truth. A transsexual has been attacked with a lie. A lie that has altered their entire life.

n (*1 Timothy 4:1*) the scripture says "*Now the Spirit expressly says that in latter times some will depart from the faith, giving heed to deceiving spirits and doctrines of demons"*. The word doctrine means teaching. Demons will teach you a lie when you refuse to receive the truth of God's word. Moreover, the life of a transsexual is filled with a diversity of complexities.

There are physical, social, emotional and legal problems to consider. The transsexual must undergo extensive physical preparation: surgery, hormone shots, alteration of appearance, charge of voice tone, manner of walking, gestures, and cross-dressing or adapting to a new wardrobe. The transsexual must adjust to social challenges: criticism, nonacceptance of new identity, prejudice, stereotyping, community injustice, employment deprivation, use of public bathrooms.

The transsexual must adjust to the emotional stress: the excruciating pain of not being accepted in their new identity role. The transsexual must prepare for legal difficulties: change of name, marriage, adoption, positions and opportunities that challenge the validation of true gender such as: sports competition that might require all male or all female competitors, and who they thought was a woman turns out to be a man.; a beauty pageant, military positions requiring a certain sex qualification. Or a sexual harassment charge not taken serious due to the argument that the victim is not really the opposite sex.

Life can become very difficult for a transsexual lifestyle. Even the preparatory stage prior to gender reassignment can be difficult. The client is asked to go through a year of total conditioning by dressing, working and living in the desired gender role. But according to *"Gender Web. Org"*, 90% of the client prospects change their mind.

Nevertheless, in spite of the perplexities surrounding the lifestyle of transsexuality, God is clear that this behavior is not the will of

God. In (*Genesis 1:27*) the scripture says, "*God created man in His own image: in the image of God, He created him: male and female He crated them.*" God created the man and woman, "*male and female.*" The different names (male and female) that he gave them indicated that God expected both people to be different. He expected the male to be a male, and the female to be a female. The etymology and meaning of the terms tell us a lot about God's intention for the male role and female role. If you notice, both terms contain the word male; female and male, because both the woman and man are males. The difference is in the physical design of the woman's body from the man's body. The woman is called female, because the root word "fe" means she was designed to carry a fetus. Likewise, the term woman means a man with a womb (wo-man.)

What the Holy Spirit is saying to us in the creative design of the man and woman, is that there is an unquestionable guideline that clearly determines the true sex gender. If you have a penis you are a man. And if you have a vagina you are a woman. It is the sex organs that indicate your God assigned gender role. Even in the rare case of a hermaphrodite; a person born with both the male and female organs. Medical experts have verified that this person is generally a female who needs to have the penis surgically removed. This person has a womb (wo-man.) A man does not have a womb. Hence, we know that such a person is without question a woman. Your sex organs determine your sexual identity.

(ADVICE)

Key Problem: If you are struggling with transsexuality; this is an issue with gender conflict. You are facing a conflict with who you are. God has already answered that question in your natural sex organs.

To overcome transsexuality, pray, and ask God to help you apply the following steps:

1. Repent- Turn away from this sin and ask God to forgive you (*Acts 3:19.*)

2. Accept your natural gender. (*Psalm 139:13,14.*)

3. Avoid any association with homosexuals, transsexuals transvestites. (*2 Corinthians 6:17.*)

4. Ministry Group- Join a men's/women's fellowship. Allow Go to help you learn to build healthy relationships. Acts 2:40-46 (*Hebrews 10:25.*)

For additional help and information See *Homosexual, Cross dre*ssing.

Voyeur

Voyeur- the act of being sexually aroused through sight. Eyes ar one of the major gates of influence. Sight has a powerful impac on the experiences of mankind. It is through what you see that yo can be powerfully persuaded to make a good decision or a ba decision.

For example, it has been noted that attractive people have an easie chance obtaining employment than people who are considere less attractive. People like the sight of beautiful things. What w see has an impact on our decisions. The principle is displayed i (*Genesis 3:6*), where the scripture says, "*So when the woma saw that the tree was good for food, that it was pleasant to th eyes and a tree desirable to make one wise she took it's fruit an ate.*" The Devil presented Eve with an object that was "*beautiful* to her eyes, and it influenced the direction of her decision.

Because God made the eyes of man, looking within itself is neve where the problem lies. And, in case you are wondering, it's oka to look at an attractive person. It reminds you that God is a wonderful artist.

However, the problem is not in when, but in how. How you look at anything in life determines whether you are right or wrong.

The problem with normal looking verses voyeurism, is the how. A voyeur has lost control on how he or she looks at another person. As I forestated in the beginning of our discussion; the eyes are major channels of the human life. Satan knew this from the very beginning of time, and still knows that this is a gate through which he can enter the human world, causing much destruction. In (*1 John 2:16*), the scriptures says, *"For all that is in the world-the lust of the flesh, the lust of the eyes, and the pride of life."* The term *"world"* in this scriptures, means *"system of evil."*

The system of evil, which Satan rules, contains *"lustful eyes."* In (*Matthew 5:28.*) Jesus said, *"Whoever looks at a woman to lust for her has already committed adultery with her in his heart."* Notice, in both scriptures, the focus is on how the eyes are being used. Because the voyeur lacks control of the eyes, there is an array of behavior ranging from abnormal stares, roving eyes, to invasion of privacy. The voyeur feeds off of images; images that could consist of women bending over, women in a short skirt, a man or woman in tight clothing, a muscular body, or just the exposure of a lot of skin. These images are secured through cameras (video, Polaroid etc.), and the most sophisticated camera of them all, the brain.

Due to the secretive nature of voyeurism, many develop into self-made spies and Peeping Toms. Speaking about the Peeping Tom, allow me to give you some short history. According to the online Encarta Encyclopedia, the legend of the Peeping Tom goes back to the Second Century, involving a woman by the name of *"Lady Godiva."* She consented to her husband to ride through town on a white horse while naked, in exchange for reducing the town taxes. During her naked ride, the town was ordered to remain indoors behind closed shutters. But, a tailor peeped through his shutters and became blind, later being known as "*Peeping Tom.*"

Because of the many images that we all face each day, anyone could be challenged by voyeurism. The solution to preventing voyeurism is in two key passages of scripture:

First, (*Job 31:1*), the Bible says, "*I have made a covenant with my eyes, why then should I look upon a young woman.*" Here, the word "*covenant*" means agreement. Job was saying, I have made an agreement to control my eyes. We must train our eyes to not look upon things, or in ways that do not promote the word of God.

Second, eyes are extensions of the mind. Your eyes do not tell you what you are looking at. Actually, it is the brain that tells you yellow from green or tall from short. Your eyes are used to see what the brain is telling it. The mind expresses itself through the eyes. Therefore, if the eyes are connected to the mind, the eyes are controlled by controlling your mind (thoughts.) The second key passage, which supports the control of our thought life, is in (*2 Corinthians 10:5*), which says, "*Casting down evil imaginations, and everything that exalts itself against the knowledge of God, bringing every thought into captivity to the obedience of Christ.*'

God wants us to constantly line our thinking up with the mind o God. Because Christ and the word of God are one in the same (*St John 1:1*), our thoughts are controlled by thinking the word o God. As we allow the word of God to control our mind, we wil take control of our eyes.

(ADVICE)

Key Problem: If you are struggling with voyeurism; this an issue with the eyes and the mind.

To overcome voyeurism, pray, and ask God to help you apply the following steps:

1. Repent- Turn away from this sin and ask God to forgive you. (*Acts 3:19.*)

2. Avoid ungodly images/pictures. (*Matthew 5:28.*)

3. Refuse ungodly thinking. (*2 Corinthians 10:5.*)

4. Fill your mind with sexual scriptures. (*1 Corinthians 6:18, Colossians 3:16, 1 Thessalonians 4:3, 2 Timothy 2:22, Matthew 5:28, Genesis 39:7-12.*)

For additional help and information See *Lust, Pornography*

Zodiac

Zodiac- a heavenly circle of the celestial bodies (sun, moon, other planets.) The Zodiac is about the positions and movements of the planets.

Astrologers have developed charts or diagrams of these planetary positions in an attempt to predict the events of someone's life, by what is better known as the horoscope. The horoscope contains 12 signs or sections of the heavenlies. It is said that astrologers have divided the heavens into 12 sections, known as the 12 sun-signs.

It is believed that the movements of the planets affect the activity of each sun-sign (Capricorn, Aquarius, Pisces, Aries, Taurus, Gemini, Cancer, Leo, Virgo, Libra, Scorpio, Sagittarius.) These are referred to as sun-signs, because the movements of the planets evolve around the sun, and are influenced by the sun's celestial power.

Moreover, it is believed that a person's sign is determined by the month they were born in. And the month or sign that they were born in, carries fixed characteristics, which have been determined by the Zodiac. For example, according to "*MSN Astrology*", the Cancer sign is said to "*crave the security of home, family and devoted relationships.*" Hence, it is believed that you can understand your life, and help determine your future by studying the Zodiac.

Astrologers believe that the Zodiac can help provide guidance and answers for the individual needs of one's life. This is why many astrologers write regular columns in the newspaper called readings. A reading is the astrologer attempting to tell you what's currently happening in your life, and what will happen (your future) based upon your sign. Which they believe is determined by the Zodiac not God. And incidentally, the Bible speaks about the positive side of the Zodiac, as declaring revelation about God. In (*Psalms 91:1*), the Bible says, "*The "heavens" declare the glory of God; and the firmament shows His handiwork.*" Notice the word "*heavens.*" This is undoubtedly a reference to the Zodiac.

We know this, because the Zodiac is about the heavenlies or planetary movements. And, this is not hard to believe, when we consider the fact that God made the heavens. However, this discussion is about the misuse of the Zodiac.

The connection that the Zodiac has with sexuality, is that there is such a strong influence on the lives of so many people, over the accuracy of the so called zodiac-horoscope, that people rely upon this horoscope to help make romantic decisions. And the question that often comes up when two people are meeting for the first time is "what's your sign?." People believe that this diagram of the Zodiac, can help them select their "soul mate."

This is indeed an expression of sexuality. But, because the Zodiac is viewed by many as a counselor, seer or life-guide, that make this type of observation of the zodiac, a sin. Because, there is only one Counselor; the Lord Jesus Christ (*Isaiah 9:6.*) There is one Seer, only God the Father can see into life, and know all things (*Hebrews 4:12,13*), and only one true Guide, the Holy Spirit (*St. John 16:13.*)

Thus, in this experience we have sex and we have sin; that turns the experience into sexual sin. In (*Isaiah 47:13*), from the "*New American Standard Translation*", the Bible says, "*You are wearied with your many counsels, Let now the astrologers, those who prophesy by the stars, those who predict by the new moons, stand up and save you from what will come upon you.*" The Spirit of God reveals in this passage that ungodly observation of the Zodiac is not new. Even in ancient times people relied upon the movement of the stars, and position of the planets to provide counsel, or direction for their life. The scripture is clear that God condemns such activity. Trust in the Zodiac as a guide for life is "*idolatry.*" An idol is anything that is treated as God. In (*Exodus 20:3*), the scripture says, "*I will have no other gods before me.*"

Moreover, it is note worthy to point out the close association between astrology and the occult. The term occult means to hide. It is the belief that there is hidden knowledge in the universe. And that this knowledge can be discovered through astrology (Zodiac), divination, magic, and spirit-beings. In (*Deuteronomy 18:10-12*), the scriptures condemn occultic practices and associations.

People who believe in the Zodiac look to it to direct life and the determine the future. God, and only God determines the future (*James 4:13-15.*)

Because people believe that the Zodiac is a reliable resource for direction, many will seek it to determine their love life. But, be advised God is the original match-maker; (*Genesis 2:22*), says, "*Then the rib which the Lord God had taken from man He made into a woman. And He brought her to the man.*" Notice, God brought Adam and Eve together, not the Zodiac.

(ADVICE)

Key Problem: If you are struggling with the Zodiac; this is an issue with idolatry. It is faith in the movements of the planets for direction of life.

To overcome misuse of the Zodiac, pray, and ask God to help you apply the following steps:

1. Repent- Turn away from this sin and ask God to forgive you. (*Acts 3:19.*)

2. Seek God to direct your life in all things. (*Proverbs 3:4,5.*)

3. Rely upon the word of God as written proof for the right decisions. (*2 Timothy 3:16.*)

4. Avoid anything that claims to do what God can do. (*Exodus 20:3.*)

STEPS TO A NEW LIFE

A. Trust Jesus Christ as your Lord and Savior; Pray the following prayer.

Dear Jesus,
I believe you died for me, and rose again on the third day.
Forgive me of my sins. I receive you as my personal Lord and
Savior. Thank you for giving me your gift of salvation! Amen

B. Immediately join a church - *Hebrews 10:25, Acts 2:40 - 46*

C. Develop a spiritual schedule:

    1. Daily Prayer - *Matthew 6:9 - 13*

    2. Daily Bible study - *2 Timothy 2:15*

    3. Regular spiritual fellowship - *Acts 2:40-46, 1 John 1:3.*

    4. Frequent fasting - *Matthew 6:16*

    5. Immediate obedience - *Deuteronomy 28:1 - 3, Matthew 4:1 - 10.*

PRAYER OF DELIVERANCE

Dear Heavenly Father,
Forgive me of my sins. I repent and turn away from [name the sin]. I command every evil spirit that entered my life through [name the sin] to go! I take the sword of the word of God, and I sever soul-ties with [name the sin, and/or person].I reclaim everything that Satan stole through sexual sin. And I surrender my spirit, mind and body to the Holy Spirit as a vessel of honor and glory.

OUR GOSPEL MISSION

To see millions accept the Lord Jesus Christ as their personal Lord and Savior; to see those who are held captive within the walls of sexual sin set free; to see multitudes restored to everything that Satan stole through sexual immorality, and to see minds renewed in the word of God by the power of the Holy Spirit. Please help us fulfill this mission, by sharing your testimony with at least one person on how God blessed you through reading this book!

DOMINION CHRISTIAN CENTER INTERNATIONAL AND MAD AGAINST SEXUAL SIN MINISTRIES

HOW TO CONTACT US:

For product information, speaking engagements, additional help, classes, questions or information:

Dominion Christian Center International

4251 Fischer

Detroit, MI 48214

313-922-1728

www.dominionintl.org

or Email:

pastorsmith@dominionintl.org

NOTES

NOTES

NOTES

NOTES

NOTES

NOTES

NOTES

NOTES

NOTES

NOTES

NOTES

NOTES

NOTES

NOTES

NOTES

NOTES

NOTES

NOTES

NOTES

NOTES

NOTES

NOTES

NOTES

NOTES

NOTES

NOTES